16 Books Smoke
WORD FLUENCY

STATE

VOCABULARY

WAYS

DIVERGENT

Different uses
for
1. Buck
2. ruler
3. button
4. glass
any object
around

1. Mary was late for dinner.

Ted was
afraid.

2. Johnny was sad.

3. Bobby was glad it was Saturday.

4. Jane's friend couldn't come over.

divergent production

A B C D E F G H I J K
L M N O P Q R S T U V W
X Y Z — Except in
better quantities.
Instant Play & learn game take words
+ make them into sentences.

interesting comments
words into
sentences

children love to come up with
different ideas.

The Structure of Intellect

Its Interpretation and Uses

The Structure of Intellect

Its Interpretation and Uses

MARY NACOL MEEKER

UNIVERSITY OF SOUTHERN CALIFORNIA

Charles E. Merrill Publishing Company
A Bell & Howell Company
Columbus, Ohio

Newell C. Kephart,

Editor

Standard Book Number: 675-09516-6

Library of Congress Catalog Card Number: 69-17296

1 2 3 4 5 6 7 8 9 10   75 74 73 72 71 70 69

The line drawings for chapter openings 3–7 are courtesy of G. Shaw.

PRINTED IN THE UNITED STATES OF AMERICA

Dedication to Everett Craig

A CREED

Open my mind's eye that I may see beyond the now.
Let me know the finest from the past.
And when no reason guides the way
   or feelings interplay with what I see,
   then lead me into right.
   Let me comfort into light.
   Help me bring the non-blind sight,
   to remove the hate which anchors fright.
Help me bear the racking ache
   I feel from hopeless human pains.
So I can walk with measured tred
   the stairs of ignorance.

Foreword

From the time that the structure-of-intellect theory was conceived, and on repeated occasions since then, I have taken advantage of each opportunity to point out the implications of that theory for education and for intelligence testing. As every educator realizes, there is a large gap between basic psychological theory and its application to educational theory and practice. Very often it requires considerable hard thinking, diligent research and exploratory development to bridge that gap. It is with a great deal of satisfaction and pleasure, then, that I write this short foreword to Dr. Meeker's contribution. She is taking notable steps to bridge the gap.

For one who has not lived on a day-to-day basis with the problems of differentiable intellectual abilities, as is true of my colleagues in the Aptitudes Research Project, Dr. Meeker's grasp of the theory and of its significance is unusual. Her application of this understanding to educational and testing problems has been able and stimulating. At this stage, she has not attempted to make thorough-going applications of the theory to the philosophy of education or to instructional procedures, but has concentrated more on curriculum development, on learning and developmental problems, and on testing with the most commonly used individual intelligence scales.

Our present knowledge of the many facets of intelligence is such as to reveal how limited is a single score, or even a pair of scores, from current intelligence scales. There is still a hiatus in our knowledge about the range of structure-of-intellect abilities in children below the fifth and sixth grades, but there is enough evidence to lead us to be sufficiently optimistic to expect most of those abilities to manifest themselves at the lower age levels. Anticipating the factor-analytic demonstration of a rather general applicability of the theory, and not wishing to wait until the needed tests of such abilities are available, Dr. Meeker has taken some important steps in attempting to make the most of standard tests now available.

Present IQ test scales fall far short of covering the potential list of abilities, but it can be recognized that some of those abilities are indicated by certain components of those scales. The contribution of those abilities to measurement are all but lost in the composite scores generally in use. Dr. Meeker proposes that such information not be lost but that it be utilized for what it may add to understanding the intellectual resources and weaknesses of individuals. Future analytical research with children such as has been so successful with adolescents and adults will answer the question of the degree of dependence to be placed upon this additional information, as Dr. Meeker realizes. It is hoped that the lead that her procedure gives to testing technology over basic science will be very much shorter than that which has been enjoyed by standard IQ tests.

J. P. Guilford

Preface

There are three discrete systems operating within education: administration, curriculum, and psychology (often called guidance). This book attempts to show a way of coordinating two of the systems so that they act as a unity, beneficial to the individual student, economical for the administration. It has been my intent to interpret a complex psychological model of intelligence for use within the existing framework of curriculum. A secondary purpose has been to show that cognitive therapy can properly be accomplished within the domain of the school where learning and social problems are most often first detected. A direction is given for planning curriculum so that individual and group strengths and deficits are discovered and taught with materials well known to the teacher. Specific ways of organizing teaching experiences to best benefit students are outlined. If the purpose of education is indeed to make changes in the knowledge fund of students, then we need to be sure that we know what the structure of expected learning is; it becomes our obligation as educators to expose students to most of these intellectual aspects.

The following points are covered: Curriculum can be rooted in a theory of intellectual functioning — the model used here is Guilford's Structure of Intellect; educational planning for students admitted to special classes can be rooted in this theory of intelligence; programmed curriculum tailored for them individually can be based on the same behavior samplings (which are strengths or deficits) in the very tests by which they are placed. Individual structure-of-intellect cells are defined and explained. Traditional educational tests which test these cells are listed for each ability and limited, but specific tasks are suggested. Means of translating Binet and WISC responses to programmed learning are given, and a very preliminary attempt to relate percept learning to concept learning is demonstrated. In the words of Francis Keppel,

> The first revolution in American education was a revolution in *quantity*. Everyone was to be provided the chance for an education of some sort. That revolution is almost won in the schools and is on its way in higher education. The second revolution is *equality* of opportunity. That revolution is under way. The next turn of the wheel must be a revolution in *quality*.

Finally, I wish to acknowledge with deep appreciation the efforts of Paul Christensen and Robert Meeker for their valuable editorial assistance and methodological organization of the manuscript. Also, I am indeed indebted to Gerri Garsh of Charles E. Merrill Publishing Co. for her insightful suggestions and actions as production editor.

Contents

PART ONE
Overview of the Structure of Intellect   1

CHAPTER 1
Introduction   3

List of Figures

List of Tables

PART ONE

Overview of the Structure of Intellect

1

Introduction

The educational psychologist is a newcomer to the school systems. He is neither an orthodox clinician nor a pure education-methods specialist; he is a child development psychologist whose knowledge is permeated with learning theory, educational practices, statistical methods of evaluation, and sociological principles. He takes his ethics from the code of the American Psychological Association, although his practice within the school systems is still currently being defined.

At present the primary function of the school psychologist is to identify sources of learning and behavior problems which handicap those students who are referred to him. The psychologist must use individual methods of appraisal to determine the student's needs which can be met as well as possible within the school environment with whatever school capacities are available.

Sometimes the problems are such that outside referral is the only answer, and for these, appropriate modifications are requested on the part of teachers and, hopefully, parents. Sometimes, however, the problems stem from cognitive deficits such as poor memory, inability to see relations, poor unit discrimination; for these, the resolution of the learning or behavior problems must be found by making appropriate modifications of curricular practices. This means that a hygienic or therapeutic approach to solving individual problems which stem from cognitive disabilities can then be achieved within the school environment by changing the task, not the subject matter, or method.

Many school professionals, and The Association of School

Psychologists and Psychometrists in California, have stated that there is a need for a new kind of education specialist—the education engineer—who would have experience with practical applications of educational principles, who would be familiar with and well trained at the theoretical level, and who would therefore reduce the lag between practice and theory in educational systems.

Structure-of-Intellect Cube

Newly developed knowledge which seems to be useful for this purpose is Guilford's Structure of Intellect (SOI). Through multivariate methods, Dr. Guilford and his associates have developed for psychology an acculturated model of intellectual aptitudes or intelligence which seems to encompass most of those abilities defining testable performances of human intellectual functioning. These abilities are found repeatedly when students' test results are factored. We should not, however, be content only with identifying those kinds of abilities students need for functioning intellectually; we should attempt also to give students experiences which will help them develop those abilities. Such an approach to education would represent a different and promising goal for education. *It would seem that teaching the ability to learn should be considered as equally important a goal as is a mastery of prescribed content.*

Unquestionably, the school psychologist's knowledge should be expanded beyond the concept of an IQ score and should include knowledge of the range of individual abilities which make up intelligence. Such knowledge not only greatly changes his concept of what intellectual performance is, but also provides a more functional bridge between measurable abilities and matters of curriculum.

The purpose of this book is to describe the Structure of Intellect as a model within which we may ascertain parameters of abilities for those individual students who come to the attention of the school psychologist. Ways are suggested by which the psychologist can improve his diagnostic skills and consequently his recommendations of help for each student. With the improvement of the psychologist's ability to make differential diagnoses, aid is given teachers to meet the students' deficits. Thus a fundamental goal of education can be achieved. The objective is to teach students *how* to learn.

Why the SOI?

In the past decade or more the American educational system has been subject to a rather critical introspective review; largely on account of the numbers in the establishment, many problems have been identified and many solutions suggested. But as with most self-analyses, there has been a strong reticence to look very profoundly into the most well-established practices. There have been some changes to strengthen and enrich the curriculum, and there have been some modifications to accelerate and streamline teaching techniques, but there has been little fundamental effect on the learning process itself. It is still conceived as the transmission of curriculum from teacher to pupil, and within this narrowly defined process there are few effective procedures for coping with individual failure. Thus, despite the best intended changes in the system, there are uneasy feelings about major educational goals both in terms of the society and the individual.

If, metaphorically, there can be institutional feelings of inadequacy, then, in a similar vein, research must stand as one of the more prevalent defense mechanisms for the educational system. The implication, as intended, is that many of the faults persist, not from lack of information but from failure to internalize some of the best knowledge already available. If the present work serves any therapeutic function, it is to facilitate this process of internalization — to make a significant body of knowledge, the structure-of-intellect (SOI) (Guilford, 1966)* model of cognitive abilities, more accessible to the educational community.

There are at least two major educational problems to which the SOI might effectively be applied. The first problem is largely philosophical in perspective and stems from the exponentially accelerating growth of subject matter itself. As the body of information continues to expand, educators are finding it increasingly difficult to keep pace. The concept of education as the transmission of curriculum from teacher to pupil is sufficient in a static or slowly evolving culture; but when the changes in curriculum approach or surpass the rate of transmission, the system either lags behind or moves toward circumventing the problem — a method which forces specialization at ever earlier stages in the process. Such is the situation today in industry and even in teaching. Prerequisites in teaching the ability to learn are necessarily means of differentiating and measuring those abilities which will become the more immediate center of attention. Again, the need is to apply that which is already in hand; the SOI analysis of intellectual abilities can serve as a basis for meeting the problem of burgeoning curriculum. Christensen (1963), one of the pioneers in SOI research, has emphasized this aspect of its potential application:

> What is not always recognized in this period of rapid change is that although situations change, task requirements change, subject matters change, and technology changes most, . . . human thinking characteristics and basic skills remain relatively the same, and we know that each individual himself varies in his abilities only within specifiable parameters.

It would seem here that implied is the possibility that abilities are somewhat fixed. The reader will wonder, of course, how one can advocate teach-

---

* The sources for all such citations can be found in the general bibliography at the end of the book.

ing (or changing) abilities in humans when they are somewhat stable and vary within specifiable parameters. The abilities described within the structure are abilities found to exist among a multitude of students, not one, for obviously many students do not possess all abilities. Secondly, in the presence of all of the expansive changes going on elsewhere, there does remain some structure in the way we can separate, describe, and measure those functions employed by humans engaging in productive intellectual activity. The *application* of our intelligence depends upon the growth of these functions (abilities). In teaching children to learn, this structure provides us with a relatively secure base upon which we can fashion learning experiences — perhaps more secure a base than "content of subject matter" presents us.

A second problem is more narrowly pedagogical than philosophical in its perspective. It is a problem most keenly felt at the basic level of the educational process, namely, how to cope with individual failure. No one feels this problem more keenly than the teacher. By and large she is successful. Since her training in methods has generally been geared to the population as a whole, her achievement by these standards is adequate even if it is less than complete. But there is little comfort in this knowledge when some students with adequate intelligence fail to learn. This situation is all the more frustrating for the teacher who generally succeeds; the exceptional cases are not testimony to her competence for they are failures by her own professional standards. She learns soon that she most probably cannot do better by merely redoubling her efforts or by improving her techniques. At this point, more than time or technique, she needs information. Why has this student failed when others of equal or of lesser measured intelligence have succeeded?

There is, of course, no single answer to this question. The potential explanations for a given case of individual failure are diverse in kind, variously related, and more or less obvious. The causes may be due to temperament; they may be familial, social, or cultural. There may be a single dominant cause or several interrelated, and even for the specialist the causes may be easily identified or difficult to detect. While no single cause can account for all failure, there is one type of explanation and attendant therapy that is most salient to the school system simply because it is wholly within the educational province. That is the area of cognitive therapy. The failure of many students can be directly attributable to the fact that they have not developed requisite abilities for success. This observation seems, at first glance, to be truistic; it is all the more ironic, then, that it has generally been neglected in the educational process.

One goal of cognitive therapy is the realization of a student's learning potential, and the process requires some measure of his abilities and some concrete means of exploiting his strengths and developing his weaknesses. This goal is well recognized — the system has long been concerned with underachievement — but the means have been left wanting because the abilities requisite for success in learning have been only vaguely understood (too

Cognitive Therapy

often left to a group IQ score) and only indirectly approached. The logically prior need, quite obviously, is one of understanding: The direct approach to a student's deficiencies is contingent upon a differentiated measure of his abilities. Differentiation is the key. The knowledge that he scores well on an intelligence test but performs rather poorly academically serves to define underachievement but does little to explain it. By contrast, with the knowledge that he is weak in, say, memory, one can deal directly with his potential source of difficulty by remediation in memory skills. Again, all of this is contingent upon a differentiated measure of intellectual abilities, and again the required knowledge is already in hand — the Structure of Intellect can provide the measure of differentiated assessment.

In the wider context of dealing with individual failure, cognitive therapy is not advanced as a cure-all; it is, instead, a new approach to learning problems. It is one, too, which is well within the charter of the educational institution. Thus, even in the cases where cognitive deficiences are rooted in deeper non-school causes, an SOI assessment provides an academically acceptable method for dealing directly, if only secondarily, with a manifest failure in the educational process.

Cognitive therapy, for all its practical saliency and patently direct approach, is not a generally well-developed practice in the educational system, although the signs that prescriptive teaching must be undertaken are well prophesied by Laurence Peter (1965) and Robert Watson (1967). Practically speaking, then, it is not altogether obvious that the failures of many students are attributable to the fact that the students have not developed requisite abilities for successful learning. Nor is it often obvious that many intellectual failures can be remedied by direct training in the prerequisite intellectual skills. The obviating component in the process is the differentiation of intellectual abilities which a model like the Structure of Intellect can provide.

The Structure of Intellect—
Research Background

The Structure of Intellect is a model of intellectual abilities. It is the product of factor-analytic research conducted by J. P. Guilford and his associates in the Psychological Laboratory at the University of Southern California.

The factor-analytic methods employed in this research are, of course, the direct outgrowth of Guilford's extensive work following that of Thurstone. Guilford's methods and the research rationale are well documented in a series of reports under the general title "Reports from the Psychological Laboratory."

The initial research for the SOI was based upon a population of young adults. Follow-up research by other investigators such as Ball, Brown, Carl-

FIGURE 1-1
STRUCTURE OF INTELLECT CUBE*

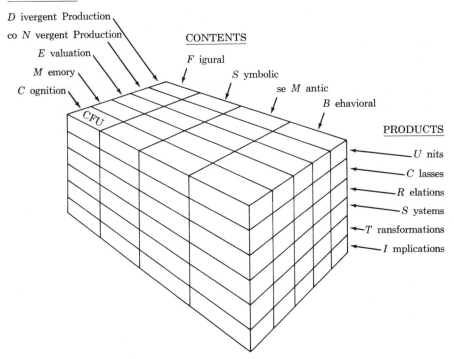

OPERATIONS

D ivergent Production

co *N* vergent Production

E valuation

M emory

C ognition

CONTENTS

F igural

S ymbolic

se *M* antic

B ehavioral

CFU

PRODUCTS

U nits

C lasses

R elations

S ystems

T ransformations

I mplications

The ideas basic to the structure-of-intellect (SOI) theory were formulated in the late 1950's following the factor analysis of many tests, and were successively refined until the present model was formulated. The model is a three-way classification of intellectual abilities designed to encompass and organize intellectual aptitude factors.

The three dimensions of the model specify first, the operation, second, the content, and third, the product of a given kind of intellectual act. Each factor hypothesized or accounted for by the model is uniquely located and defined by specifying a category on each of the three dimensions. The three categories that specify each factor are coded in terms of a trigram symbol specifying the Operation, Content, and Product, respectively, for the factor. For example, reading clockwise—CFU stands for *C*ognition of a *F*igural *U*nit. The letters employed as codes together with definitions of the dimensions and their categories are described in subsequent chapters. A glossary appears at the end of the book.

---

*From J. P. Guilford (1966), Report 36, USC. The locations of structure labels have been changed, with permission from Dr. Guilford, so as to facilitate reading the trigrams from left to right.

son, Loeffler, McCartin, Meeker, Meyers, Orpet, Ridler, Sitkei, Stott, Tenopyr, Torrance, Watts, among others, has substantiated the original findings
with subject populations ranging in age from two through fifteen years. It is
this validation on school-age children which provides the general rationale
for using the structure-of-intellect model in the area of primary and secondary education.

An Overview of the Model

The Structure of Intellect conceptualizes intellectual abilities in a three-
dimensional model (FIG. 1-1). Every intellectual ability in the structure is
thus characterized in terms of the type of operation which is employed, the
content involved, and the sort of product which results. Complete characteri-
zation of an intellectual ability is achieved in terms of the possible subclass
differentiation on each of the three major dimensions. "Operations" is differentiated five ways: Memory, Cognition, Evaluation, Divergent Production,
and coNvergent Production. Figure 1-2 demonstrates the breaking apart of
the major slices (operations) of the matrix cube. Contents and Products are
identical components in each of the major operations. "Contents" is differentiated by four subclasses: Figural, Symbolic, seMantic, and Behavioral.
"Products" is differentiated by six subcategories: Units, Classes, Relations,
Systems, Transformations and Implications. The complete schema is represented by a three-dimensional classification array of 120 predicted cells or
categories of intellectual abilities.

Figure 1-3 removes the third-dimensional perspective and shows the
separation of the five operations so that it is a graphic profile of the structure on a flat plane.

Thus the 120 distinct types of intellectual abilities are derived from the
intersection of the three-way classification scheme. Conversely, a unique
definition can be obtained for each cell by simply specifying its characteristics in terms of the three major dimensions.

A few conventions are useful in dealing with the resultant complexity of
120 distinct types of intellectual abilities. Each cell in the array is tagged
with a trigram that readily identifies its three-way subclassification. "MFU"
stands for *Memory* of *Figural Units*; "CSC" stands for *Cognition* of *Symbolic
Classes*; and so on. Each ability is thus tagged according to the initial letters
of its operations-contents-products categorization; there are only two exceptions to this procedure — in order to provide distinction between cognition
and convergent-production processes, the convention uses C for Cognition
and N for Co-N-vergent Production; secondly, in order to distinguish symbolic and semantic contents, the convention uses S for Symbolic and M for
Se-M-antic; otherwise first-letter combinations provide unique shorthand
names for each ability.

The "cube" is simply a visual aid to conceptualizing the three-way classification and is convenient for depicting the intellectual abilities as delineated

FIGURE 1-2
STRUCTURE OF INTELLECT

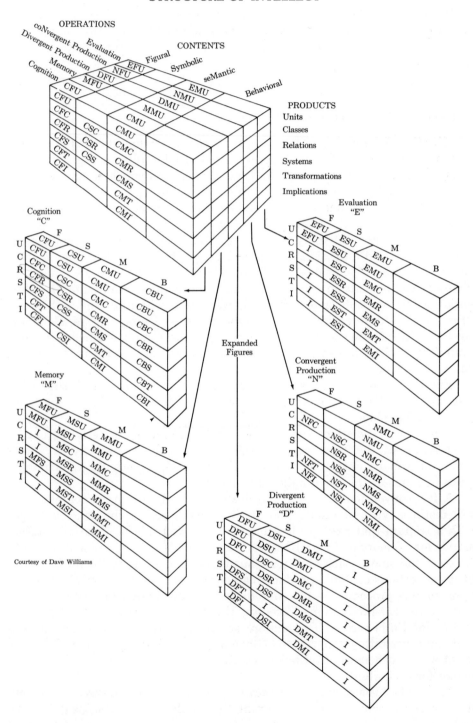

Courtesy of Dave Williams

This one

FIGURE 1-3
STRUCTURE OF INTELLECT
A Flow Diagram of the Processes

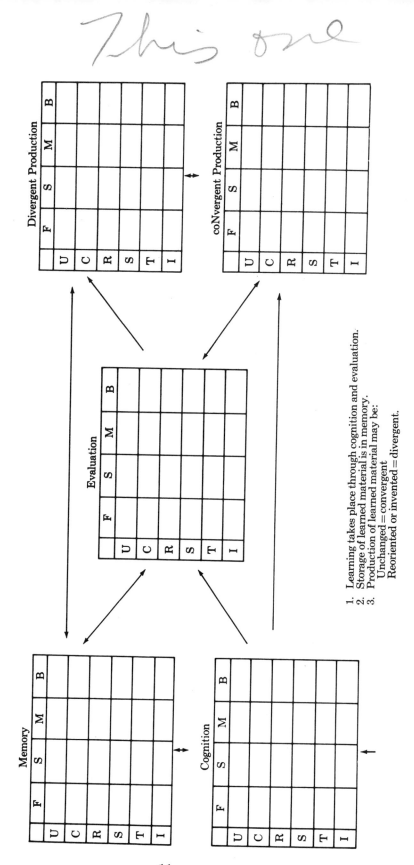

1. Learning takes place through cognition and evaluation.
2. Storage of learned material is in memory.
3. Production of learned material may be:
   Unchanged = convergent
   Reoriented or invented = divergent.

11

multivariate analyses of measured performance. The Structure of Intellect implies nothing beyond this conceptualization. Neither should any implication be drawn from the fact that there is a conventional order (operations-contents-products) used in naming the various abilities. The order is strictly conventional; that is, no priority — logical or psychological, developmental or hierarchical — is intended either within or between the categories of classification. These remarks are pertinent to the research of the SOI; for, by contrast, the user of the SOI will find it difficult to suspend judgment of speculation completely — to refrain from all off-hand speculations — about the various categories in their relationship to the dynamics of the learning process. The reader should be aware that these speculations tendered throughout the exposition are adjunct to and not part of the formal SOI model.

2

The Major Dimensions
and Subcategories

This section describes the major dimensions and subcategories of the SOI model. The intention here, as throughout, is to interpret the SOI to the school psychologist and the classroom teacher. To this end Chapter 2 introduces the major dimensions and their subcategories by presenting definitions together with commentary that relate the precise but very general definitions to the specific concerns of educational practice.*

Operations:
Major kinds of intellectual activities or processes; things the organism does with the raw materials of information, information being defined as 'that which the organism discriminates.'

Five major operations have been identified: Cognition, Memory, Divergent Production, coNvergent Production, and Evaluation. Each of these will be discussed in turn, but some general comments about their interrelation is pertinent at this point. For the reader encountering the SOI for the first time, there is perhaps difficulty in comprehending that the operations being identified are statistically separable processes. The difficulty, if it occurs, is most probably due to the reader's being able to see relations of logical and psychological priorities between these different intellectual activities. For

---

* The definitions in this chapter are reproduced intact from J. P. Guilford and R. Hoepfner, "Structure-of-Intellect Tests and Factors," *Reports from the Psychological Laboratory,* No. 36, 1966.

example, it is apparent that memory is contingent upon prior cognition—it would seem reasonable that one must discern information before storing it. In the dynamics of the learning process this may certainly be so, but for the methods of factor analysis this relationship (apparent or actual) is essentially irrelevant. The method requires only that test items be so constructed that the abilities emerge as statistically separable. To the researcher who constructs these test items, the priority, if real, may actually present problems in obtaining the desired purity of assessment. In other words, the supposed psychological priority may make separable assessment difficult but it need not preclude it. Fortunately, those who *use* the results of such research do not have to be concerned with these aspects of factor clarity; they may, however, face a similar but less demanding task when they construct training materials designed primarily for the exercise of any single operation. For instance, this is so when it is necessary to devise materials which strengthen memory skills without taxing the cognition ability of the student. Aspects of this type of problem will be discussed specifically in subsequent sections.

Finally, in terms of general introduction to this section, it should be noted that the Guilford tests are group administered, paper-and-pencil types. This means that the mode of decoding is almost exclusively visual; consequently, the operations are almost all implicitly visual in character. In other words, as based on assessment method, the various operations are almost uniformly (undifferentially) visual in mode of presentation although the activity elicited may or may not be visual-motor. Three minor but notable exceptions will be dealt with as the different operations are described.

Cognition: *Immediate discovery, awareness, rediscovery, or recognition of information in various forms; comprehension or understanding.*

Cognition is perhaps the most obvious of all the operations. It is certainly an essential in the education process even from the earliest stages. In terms of the dynamics of learning it seems to be the primary process since every other activity presupposes perception and awareness of stimuli with the associated ability to discriminate or attend. Without registration there would seem to be no content for further processing.

Obvious as it may be, cognition is worthy of comment as a separate ability since, despite this fact, it may actually be slighted in the classroom. The difficulty for education personnel is that they have long become accustomed to the testing of comprehension as contrasted with its exercise. It is interesting to ask teachers these questions: How often do we teach children just to comprehend? How often do we provide experiences that have as a simple goal, pure comprehension, without questions, testing, or other demands? Recreational television viewing does just this. Perhaps that is why it is so popular with children. It makes no demands on the child at all and places no pressure on him; the child can enjoy television as a spectator; he can simply comprehend, be stimulated, and take pleasure in cognition.

If almost all information taken in has to be comprehended or cognized before it can be manipulated, then children would need to experience many opportunities for tasks which require only that they do simple comprehending, that they be stimulated or intrigued. This kind of experience should be as integral a part of the curriculum at the elementary and secondary levels as it is at the kindergarten level, for it stimulates interest and motivation and thus increases visual and auditory attending. So much of our teaching is tinged with the concept that if something is taught it ought to be learned, and this can be determined only if it is tested. To the child, translated, it means he has to pay for just about everything he learns because he will be tested on it somehow, either by questions or written performance. If one of our goals is to teach students how to learn, then we need to make *some* learning enjoyable, "free of charge," and unpressured. We cannot expect young children to generalize to liking-to-learn unless learning has been made pleasurable for them at some time. Preferably this should occur in the early grades (if a choice must be made) so that if affect tinges conditioning, then learning capitalizes on a good beginning.

When the teacher presents material for intrigue, the child is free to interact in his own manner with the material and *perhaps* the result may well be that, with his teacher's appreciating his interest, he develops a self-appreciation which increases positively his self-concept. The teacher is freed academically because she can stimulate without feeling bound to test the student to determine whether or not she has accomplished her goal, and the child thus freed is motivated. He finds learning exciting because he can be stimulated through interest in spite of the fact that he is "in school."

The suggestion here for the child whose cognition is poor is that his curriculum should at first consist of twenty minutes of individual "comprehension tasks" daily if he is expected to catch on or catch up.

Modes of cognition are important in educational practice. As noted earlier, the tests from which the model was derived were almost all visual in character. In terms of school psychology it is important to note that the cognitive abilities can be further differentiated; besides the visual, there are other modes of cognition such as the auditory, kinesthetic-tactile, and olfactory. This fact is important because, as every classroom teacher recognizes, there are individual differences with regard to cognition itself. Some students are "visually minded" to the extent that they never comprehend a point until it is presented visually while others are auditory learners who seem to perform best with verbal presentation and do poorly on visually presented tasks. Frequently these auditory learners are also poor spellers (Meeker, 1966). In still other cases, particularly in research on blind and neurologically impaired populations, but not so confined, presentation is often most effective in the kinesthetic mode. In short, especially for educational applications, there is need for further refinements in the SOI model, where possible, to accommodate these important modal differences. For our immediate purposes this means only that we be alerted to modal distinctions in presentation of materials. The auditory and kinesthetic modes, especially, should receive recognition along with the visual modes in primary learning. Guilford and his associates have not been unaware of these distinctions; in at least two instances of cognition they have produced separate auditory and visual factors for the same cell; similar distinctions have been found by Mc-Carthy and Kirk (1963), and Meeker (1966). This merely serves to underscore the general point that our conception of cognition should not be limited by the accidental fact that practical considerations in education for testing purposes have demanded that the majority of the presented materials be in the visual mode.

The same type of practical consideration is also operative in the classroom; there, too, the predominant mode of presentation is visual, largely because it is the easiest way of presenting material to a group. Visual reception alone may not be sufficient if the class is composed of learners who integrate knowledge better in some other mode. On the other hand, directions to the class for the visual tasks are usually given vocally and only once. The capable child who has a short auditory memory span or limited auditory vocabulary comprehension is indeed penalized from the beginning of his school career.

Memory: *Retention or storage, with some degree of availability, of information in the same form it was committed to storage and in response to the same cues in connection with which it was learned.*

Memory, like cognition, is a well-known intellectual operation — well known in the sense that it is one of the oldest. Memory is also universally and historically recognized as a primary mental function, but it is something of an enigma in terms of our understanding how it functions in the dynamics of the learning process. We know that the organism is not restricted to the informational field of his immediate awareness, and we know that there are limitations on his ability to retrieve information from past experiences, but we do not know what underlies the retention or what accounts for the limitations. Our understanding is largely restricted to measures of the manifest ability; we have assessed memory in terms of the amounts of information that can be reproduced as qualified by the elapsed time from input to retrieval and the mode of reproduction. We have been able to distinguish degrees of long-term (retention) and short-term (immediate) memory in terms of recall (reproduction without overt cues) and recognition (reproduction or selection with overt cues presented). These distinctions have recently been further qualified in terms of the mode of initial decoding (input) of the information. At least with respect to short-term memory the auditory and visual modes of input have been identified as separate abilities (Meeker, 1966). In short, though we know considerably less about the underlying processes, we have made some important distinctions about manifest memory abilities.

This very general outline of the memory abilities has been drawn both to provide perspective for the SOI tests of the memory factors and to suggest resources for applications in the educational system.

First it should be noted, as with cognition, that the SOI does not differentiate within the memory operation in this case, both with respect to mode of input and lapsed time to retrieval. Again, for reasons of practicality in test administration, the majority of SOI research has been confined to short-term memory of visually presented materials, but our *use* of the concept need not be thus confined. We know, on the basis of other research, that memory can be further differentiated and, being aware of memory's particular saliency in education, we can reasonably assume that these distinctions can profit the school psychologist and the teacher.

It would be hard to overestimate the importance of memory abilities in the education process, especially in terms of the measured achievement which often stands as a measure of the educational system itself. It is ironic, then, that exploration of memory, and most specifically the remediation of poor memory, has largely been neglected both by planning in curriculum and by research in educational psychology. If anything, the trend has been away from memory training. The traditional method in which all students were required to memorize poems, passages, and lists of facts largely for the sake of memorization is now out of vogue, probably because the tasks were too negatively charged with emotion and frustration to be effective as memory training. While this is sufficient reason for extinction of the practice, we have little in its stead; certainly there are no well-articulated procedures for the identification of memory weakness or memory deficits and their correlations with various subject matters, or for accompanying procedures for remediation. Yet there is nothing in the literature to suggest that memory cannot be approached more directly, that we could not devise (and present in challenging, stimulating fashion) materials which exercise the memory without taxing cognition, that we cannot strengthen an auditory memory deficiency by building on a visual memory proficiency or vice versa. In short, there is strong indication that we have neither explored nor developed some of the most promising avenues in an absolutely essential area of academic learning.

Evaluation: *Reaching decisions or making judgments concerning criterion satisfaction (correctness, suitability, adequacy, desirability, etc.) of information.*

Evaluation implies a kind of sensitivity to error or discrepancy on the one hand and, on the other, a judgment of relative nearness of a number of items of information for any kind of product to a kind of model item of information on the same continuum—the ability to make judgments in relationship to known or understood standards.

The key, obviously, is "judgment," with all of the subtleties connoted by that term. Judgments may be more or less precise depending on the character of the standard or criterion. When the criterion is a well-defined principle or algorithm, the judgment has all the determinant character of a "solution." When the criterion is a working rule or is heuristic, the judgment has the character of a decision based on means-ends relationship— a matter of seeing what works and how well—not a determinant solution but at least some of the process. When the criterion is a social norm or esthetic standard, the judgment has a character that can be most readily described as a combination of social-awareness, personal-commitment, and belief-maintenance. There are, in short, many colorations of judgment depending upon the character of the criterion. In addition, there are many gradations in the clarity of the relationship between the judgmental material and the standard by which it is being judged, so that an important aspect of the process is the ability to see the connections (logical or causal) or perhaps, most characteristically, to reason by analogy.

Evaluation typically has an uneven role in the classroom. In formal education we obviously favor the exercise of "solution" type judgments. Informally, the school situation represents an important if not primary introduction to the evaluations that involve social norms and, to a lesser degree, local esthetic standards. Evaluations of the "decision-making" type are perhaps the most slighted of all. This is somewhat surprising when one considers one of the basic American philosophical foundations of the current system. Dewey, pragmatism, and the associated reliance on means-ends relationships would seem to presage greater emphasis on practical evaluations; the fact that this emphasis has not been manifest in the curriculum is undoubtedly attributable to problems of pedagogy. Direct, formal teaching of practical evaluation presents difficulties, partly because the process itself is so little understood, but also because of conflict in social value systems. With other abilities where our understanding of the process is not any more complete, we have effectively circumvented the difficulty by measuring performance in terms of output. This technique provides us with a means of evaluating our own teaching or training efforts—a comforting source of reassurance— but in the process of evaluation where the output is less precise and more indeterminate, the solace of measurement is practically precluded, so this area is slighted. Nevertheless we all make the assumption that students know how to evaluate, and that they do so from the same value system as that of the educator.

Difficult as this situation is there are ways of coping with it. Evaluation activities that are not themselves evaluated could be used on a limited scale. Closer to the more comfortable mode of measurable performance one could devise "how to" exercises: What is the best way of getting from here to New York (California)?—with alternatives depicting walking, auto, rail, airplane, . . . , and the explicit need for the student to provide his interpretation of "best." Or in an exercise of compound means-ends relationships one might elicit answers to innumerable questions which begin with: "what else could have been done?" Generally the resourceful teacher can do much toward teaching decision-making skills even though they are imprecise, poorly-defined, and hard to communicate.

The need is obviously there. When the training is left to informal methods, the deficiencies are most manifest with those who have the weakest informal resources, the disadvantaged or those generally who come from problem or rigid environments. We know that the milieu of the child can be barren* of evaluation experiences, and though we as educators cannot change the greater part of his environs we can provide formal exercise in those processes which he has no opportunity to assimilate informally.

> **Convergent Production:** *Generation of information from given information, where the emphasis is upon achieving unique or conventionally accepted best outcomes. It is likely the given information (cue) fully determines the response.*

Convergent production is "rigorous thinking"—the process of finding the answer where "finding" is something more than mere retrieval and "the answer" suggests that the domain is so systematic, ordered, and determinant that there are rules or principles for converging on the solution.

Convergent production is the most familiar SOI ability expected in schools; it is almost synonymous with curriculum assimilation. So much of the curriculum exercises this ability that it is fondly dubbed the "school block." Problem-solving tasks are staple commodities in almost all of the standard intelligence tests where the answers are preordained. Educational personnel are well acquainted with the type of curricular activities designed to elicit these analytic skills and the testing thereof, even though they may not label the activity convergent production. We do, of course, with this process as with the others, measure performance by the output, and because the answer is unique, we assume that there is a close correspondence between a correct response and the processes that converge on it. This assumption can be misleading, for if the student has previously encountered this problem or a highly similar one, he may be retrieving rather than generating the solution. Teachers and psychometrists recognize this as a practical problem and have devised techniques for this aspect of practice or rehearsal effects. Protection of standard tests, the use of alternate forms, and sufficient variation from practice to test and from teaching to tests, are all ways of precluding direct retrieval. Direct recall of a specific answer to a specific problem is but one aspect of "practice effect;" there is another aspect which is much more interesting theoretically and much more promising pedagogically. It is that humans can apparently retain the process of convergence in somewhat generalized form, an ability that permits them to learn from prior experience so that they do not have to approach each new problem *de novo*. We know this fact descriptively; we have evidence that practice in convergent-production skills is profitable, even though the mechanisms of learning dynamics which underlie this procedure remain obscure. That people do not have to start from scratch with each different problem seems to imply an ability to derive and store strategies for convergent thinking which, by implication, would involve

---

* "Barren" applying equally to economic deprivation, over-protectiveness, or an autocratic upbringing where the child has no opportunity for decision making.

evaluation and memory at a meta level. All of these observations are, of course, highly speculative and are offered not as guidelines for practitioners but rather to underscore the fact that even though education has emphasized the exercise of convergent-production abilities almost to the exclusion of other intellectual abilities, the dynamics of the processing are neither well understood nor easy to crystallize for research.

Divergent Production: *Generation of information from given information, where the emphasis is upon variety and quality of output from the same source. Likely to involve what has been called transfer. This operation is most clearly involved in aptitudes of creative potential.*

Two aspects of the formal definition are most outstanding on first encounter. One is the obvious contrast with convergent production, and the other is the implied association of this ability with creative endeavors.

The immediate contrast between convergent and divergent production is the difference between zeroing in and expanding out. The two in this respect are strikingly different abilities; but beyond this most ostensible difference there are some similarities. One such similarity is the use of principle or rule; in the case of convergent production, guided or orderly procedure is so well recognized that it might be considered axiomatic; in the case of divergent production, the need for orderly procedure is perhaps not so obvious, but a little reflection convinces us of its importance. Divergent generation does not proceed willy-nilly; the divergent thinker is not a scatterbrain; the worthwhile generation of information requires discipline and guidance. This is reflected in the formal definition in the reference to "quality." Since, once again, we do not understand the dynamics of the process, we tend to characterize it by inference from the manifestations of the activity, that is, the output of the process. In these terms we are left with a paradox: On the one hand divergent production should show fluency, flexibility, and individuality, an ability to break away from the conventional; but on the other hand it should also show quality, relevance, and discipline, an ability to stay within "reasonable" bounds. The first contrasts rather sharply with convergent production; the second suggests that some of the underlying mechanisms for the two are highly related if not identical; and, in sum, the seeming paradox of the conjunction reflects our relative understanding of the whole process.

The second aspect of divergent production that is most intriguing is its close association with creativity. Perhaps the desire for adequate measures of creativity has prompted some to equate divergent production with creativity; the association is close, but most investigators would maintain a distinction between the two. The most conservative analysis would consider divergent production as a necessary, though not sufficient, condition for creative activity; so even on this account, encouragement of this ability would represent a promising avenue to the development of creativity.

Emphasis on divergent thinking has recently been incorporated in the curriculum of some individual schools, and school personnel have generally been alerted to the importance of developing creative abilities. If the present program has deficiencies, that fact is symptomatic of our lack of understanding of the process itself along with inadequate implementation techniques. Without laying fault to any source but this, we find it is more and more apparent that the initial break with tradition has tended to stress the novel and individualistic aspect with relatively little attention to quality, relevance, and discipline. Adjustment to this enthusiastic beginning most probably lies in the direction of making divergence more productive and providing or eliciting more structure in the originality and flexibility that we seek to nurture. Since many psychologists are researching the divergent area, attendant problems may be worked out.

In closing this general description of divergent production, we may comment briefly on the matter of individual propensities toward intellectual styles. Although the question of personality style has not arisen in relation to cognition, memory, or evaluation types of students, there has been speculation by educators about whether there is any natural inclination toward convergent-production types as opposed to divergent-production types. Work by Hudson (1966), in England, has been summarized in a small book describing this typology as his personal discovery resulting from observation. Since, logically, the two are not mutually exclusive, the answer from this perspective is simply that one or the other of these abilities need not be favored.* From another point of view we know empirically that for a given individual, there will most likely be a preference for one proficiency over another, so that in terms of demonstrated ability, he might be "type-cast" as one sort or the other even when he is equally proficient in divergent and convergent productivity. Still another interpretation of this question relates abilities to interests and motivation: Do people prefer convergent-production tasks to divergent-production tasks regardless of respondents' demonstrated proficiency? The answer, according to recent research, is "yes." That in itself is not so surprising, but this same research shows relatively little relationship between interest and proficiency, and that fact is counterintuitive since we would expect people to prefer that which they do best (Merrifield, 1963; Barron, Frank, 1965). The proposed explanation of these results holds implications for the schools because it is suggested that, generally, the curriculum is so confined or undifferentiated with respect to variety of tasks that the functional association between a student's life-style and his academic pursuits may be reduced to a minimum. Taking this tentative explanation at face value, it may be concluded that the intellectual

---

* Those people who tend to make this separate identification also tend to call divergency creativity. The body of knowledge coming from investigations into aspects of creativity is so voluminous that it suggests precluding such a restricted view, and, in fact, the dimensional abilities of *Transformations* and *Implications* in any operation are also frequently found to typify "creative" people.

inclinations of "naturally" different types of thinkers are not being differentially served by the educational system, that the vitality of intrinsic motivation is not being capitalized upon, and that the end goal of education (preparation for adult role) does not include those jobs in which divergent problem solving is a most prime requisite.

Contents:
Broad classes or types of information discriminable by the organism.

Figural.   If they are figural, they may be shown as shapes like trees, forms, or concrete objects, etc., and most of them would be cognized or comprehended as visual or kinesthetic forms or totalities. Thus we have Cognition (comprehension) of a Figural object (CF—) of some kind which distinguishes it from other impinging stimuli.

Symbolic.   If the stimulus material is cognized in the form of a numeral or a single letter, or a note of music or a code symbol; this kind of stimulus distinguishable from a figural one, is called a symbol. A person can comprehend that a tree (F) differs from a number (S), thus cognizing numerals (CS—) differs from (CF—), cognizing figural stimuli.

Semantic.   The third kind of stimulus material which the organism must cognize separately from the figural and symbolic is the seMantic, labeled (M) . (The stimulus materials, called contents, are always associated as the second letter in the trigraph labeling each cell. Also, contents are identical internal components in each of the major abilities.) (See FIG. 1-3.) Cognition of seMantics would be labeled (CM—), Memory for seMantics (MM—), Evaluation of seMantics (EM—) . . . .

SeMantics (M) refer to words and ideas where an abstract meaning is so associated in the individual's repertoire of knowledge that its external referent calls up the internally associated stored word. As you read the word TREE, it has meaning and is semantic. For the infant (if he perceives it at all), TREE would not be termed semantic until he associated the word tree with the object whether it was present or not. TREE, for him, would probably be a figural stimulus, as perceived visually; if he understood the sound TREE and conjured an image TREE, the stimulus would still be Figural.

A primary teacher might well expand her goals to include teaching the student to recognize and be familiar with classification of stimuli in this manner, not only to alert him to differentiating and distinguishing figural, symbolic, and semantic items from each other in his environment, but also to teach him a rudimentary classification.

Behavioral.   The fourth content, Behavioral (B), is perhaps the most intriguing from the psychologist's point of view. Behavior is both a manifestation of a response and a stimulus. Only a few of the behavioral cell abilities have been identified and thus present a new dimension yet to be clarified and yet to be factored within the SOI model. The cognition of behavior, the evaluation of behavior, and the convergent production of behavior, once separately testable by means of structure-of-intellect tests, will in the future offer additional refinement in psychological tools.

Products:
The organization that information takes in the organism's processing of it.

Looking at the left margin of any operational matrix (FIG. 1-3), one sees horizontal lines which subdivide that dimension into different kinds of Products. Products act as organizational categories for figural, symbolic, and semantic contents or stimulus materials. Contents are organized according to the way in which the organism has processed them as products.

U—Units.   Figures, for example, can be processed singly, in which case it is a unit which is being perceived; that is, one figure, or one symbol, or a single word or idea is a unit.

Vocabulary, which is one of the most heavily loaded components in almost any IQ test, is really only one of the 120 possible kinds of abilities, CMU, or Cognition of a seMantic Unit. Certainly comprehending the meaning of a word is a more complex task than discriminating a single figure or a single numeral. CMU is more complex than CSU (Cognition of a Symbolic Unit)—discerning whether or not certain letters correctly spell a word (fair or fiar); one might be tempted to place the contents in a hierarchy from simple to complex. However, placing value judgments on tasks would defeat the purpose of a model born through the technique of factor analysis; that is, the cells represent differentiated abilities. Whether any one cell is more complex or better esteemed as a skill should be answered only on a differential basis depending on the person, the need, and the situation. A Unit, then, is any single item, one of a kind.

C—Classes.   On the other hand, however, there is a hierarchy inferred in the products dimension, for in a sense each subsumes the preceding one. For example, classes follow units. It is valid to suppose that before one can make classifications or perform a classifying task, one would have to perceive the units to be classified. Here, again, the two kinds of processes, classifying figure, symbols, or semantics ("C") and discriminating individual figures, symbols, and semantics ("U"), factor as different abilities. As will be seen in a later chapter, different profiles of students indicate variously that some can classify and not perceive units correctly; these may be examples of either the vagaries of human abilities, the minor correlation of abilities, or more simply, the achievement of the goal of a task.

It is, therefore, safer to be concerned with the ability to classify— whether it is cognition of classes of figures, symbols, or semantics, or memory for classes of figures, symbols or semantics, or for convergent pro- duction, divergent production, or evaluation of these classes. These are all independent, separate tasks representing different kinds of abilities.

R—Relations. Following Classes, reading down the left side of the Cognition square (FIG. 1-3) is the relations dimension. The individual is asked to process relations or connections between the content involved— relations between figures, or between symbols as in deciphering a code, or relations between words or ideas (semantics). Any number of work sheets can be devised, both by psychologist and by teacher, to teach children to conceptualize relations.

Many of the materials developed for the Montessori schools teach rela- tional aspects. One example is a set of wooden cylinders in which varied materials are sealed. When the child rattles them he is asked to match two that sound alike. An auditory task is involved here when the student is asked, and at the same time he is being taught, to discriminate auditory differences — a task which can be accomplished successfully only if he under- stands the differences in relationships such as loud and heavy and loud and soft or high and deep so that he can match similar sounds. Kinesthetic tasks and olfactory tasks can be devised as well. Many items in high-school group IQ tests are almost exclusively relationship tests—relations between sequences of numerals or geometric figures. Some tests actually formulate the student's score into an IQ score, yet relations between figures is the only ability being tested. The IQ score goes into the record as a permanent indi- cation of the student's academic potential, and counseling judgments are made accordingly. Suffice it to say that intelligence is much more compli- cated than a single IQ score based on results of any one or two abilities or any one test result.

S—Systems. The next dimension down (FIG. 1-3), proceeding vertically, and looking across, is that of systems. Systems may be composed of figures, symbols, or semantics. A system can be mathematical, as in arithmetic, or composed of numerals written as words where the subject must comprehend the idea of a sequence of arithmetic operations necessary for solution. Understanding the system of linguistics in sentence building (example: diagramming sentences) involves understanding the structure of language with verbs, nouns, etc., and would represent a seMantic System (—MS).

In the behavioral dimension the systems ability in cognition, for instance, involves comprehending a social situation or sequences of social events involving thoughts and feelings of persons. One test at the systems level uses pictures and cartoons to depict series of those events.

T—Transformations. Tranformation is the next kind of product; it labels a more abstract ability. If a task requires that redefinitions or modifications of the existing information be made into other information, it means that the person is in some way transforming the original material. This kind of ability may demand visual, auditory, abstract, or motor flexibility and has been found to characterize people who have been termed creative. Very young children, as compared with older children, often find that their actions in this dimension gain more acceptance and so they have more opportunities for explorations in transformation than older children. Very few opportunities at this level of functioning are allowed children once they have been enrolled in school; children often find that such action, previously acceptable, is no longer acceptable. Students are expected to learn material as it is presented, in the form in which it is presented, and any transformation a student makes may warrant an unsatisfactory reaction such as a poor mark by the teacher or laughter from the students.

Each of the contents can be transformed. Figural stimuli lend themselves more readily to transformations such as are found in puzzles, paper folding, and spatial visualization tasks. These latter tests compose some of the performance subtests in the Wechsler Intelligence Scale for Children (WISC). It is difficult to develop tests of transformation of a symbol and even more difficult to determine adequate standards of judgment so that pure factor tests can be made.

An example in the semantic dimension, however, can be given: Seeing similarities between words either in meaning or sounds, or constructive changes in existing conceptual institutions of laws or in linguistics. Clever endings to stories fall in the semantic category, especially when the ending transforms the original intent or description of the story.

I—Implications. The final and most abstract ability category across the model is implications. The ability to foresee consequences involved in figural problems can be demonstrated visually, vocally, or by motor expression. Maze tracing, a task most commonly found in IQ tests, is testing the ability to see implications in figural material.

Teaching for implications poses a challenge. It is often taken for granted that the student will see the implications of what he has learned, and he is invariably expected to generalize to unlike situations. The student or adult who does this easily is fortunate, but the one who cannot needs to be shown or taught. He is often described as "literal minded" because the teacher finds that he needs almost constant help in going from one step in learning to the next. He does not easily perceive cause and effect and eventually may come to the erroneous conclusion that he is "dumb," when actually he is simply deficient in one cognitive dimension, implications.

Learning theorists know, for instance, that if they want a student to learn a fact, they must teach that fact to him; they do not wait for generalizations to spread unless, of course, they are experimenting with the phenomenon. One technique for teaching implications is an assignment wherein problems are given to the student for alternate solutions. Another technique is one where problems are made up by the student (CMI). Another involves symbolic thinking, where scrambled numerals or letters can be organized in a specified way—where there is no alternative. The "water" problems in the Binet are good examples of tests of this ability. The child must comprehend that if he wants three measures of water and has only a five- and a two-measure measuring can, he must fill the five-measure can and pour its contents into the two-measure can—thus leaving the three he wants.

At the figural level, the making of a meaningful drawing out of squiggles will allow young children to explore figural implicative thinking. If they are then allowed to write or tell a story about their drawing, showing how the picture solved a problem, they experience semantic implications.

The preceding sections have described the general properties of each major operation, qualities of the contents, and definitions of the products. The purpose was to explicate conceptualizations behind the model. Guilford, in his book, *The Nature of Human Intelligence* (1967), treats these conceptualizations extensively, precisely, and in detail.*

---

* Less detailed but specific definitions are included in a glossary for ready reference in the back of this book.

PART TWO

Operations and Descriptions of Components

FIGURE 3-1
FACTORS IDENTIFIED IN COGNITION

	Figural	Symbolic	seMantic	Behavioral
Units	CFU V CFU A	CSU V CSU A	CMU	CBU
Classes	CFC	CSC	CMC	CBC
Relations	CFR	CSR	CMR	CBR
Systems	CFS	CSS	CMS	CBS
Transformations	CFT	(I) *	CMT	CBT
Implications	CFI	CSI	CMI	CBI

*Currently being investigated

3

Cognition Factors

Introduction

The following five chapters will describe factors in each operation. Definitions and explanations for each factor will include descriptive tests and curriculum suggestions. The behavioral dimension will not be described except where factored. Each factor cell will be described in three ways: first, a general definition of the given ability; second, wherever possible, the description will be related to psychometric materials widely used in educational measurement; and third, suggested curriculum practices for the training of that ability will be explicated. The description is thus organized so that the many differentiated abilities can be most readily assimilated by readers with stronger psychometric or curriculum background. In this sense the intended description is an ideal which could not be realized in the most comprehensive sense; some limitations are obviously required. The tests cited are restricted largely to the best-known and most frequently used tests in educational institutions, although in some isolated instances less commonly used references are given because they are available for specific tasks.

The two sections following the definition of each separate ability are entitled *Tests* and *Curriculum Suggestions*. Since these chapters are meant to be used as a quick and easy reference, neither section is fully expounded upon nor intended to be comprehensive. The factor tests are listed first. There are, of course, other tests which include or touch upon separate abilities, and if more exact coverage of the many tests in print is desired, this may be found either in Buros' *Mental Measurements Year-books* or in other texts such as Anastasi's *Psychological Testing.*

Factor tests which measure each ability are described first. Their exact definitions are taken from Report No. 36 (Guilford and Hoepfner, 1966), and each test is followed by a reference number as cited in the report. The legend for explaining citations appears below.

The curriculum suggestions are just that—simple suggestions pointing out directions and serving as models. The simplicity should, it is hoped, allow teachers to adapt subject matter both to the theoretical framework of the Structure of Intellect and to individual needs of pupils.

The descriptions are intended as suggestive explications of a given ability rather than a compendium of assessment and teaching practices.

Materials are drawn from general school experience with specific references to some of the better-known special training practices.

Legend for Factor Tests.   Tests that are numbered were designed by the Aptitudes Research Project, Department of Psychology, at the University of Southern California, Los Angeles. The number indicates the *Report from the Psychological Laboratory* in which it is described. The sources of various tests are given in terms of the following abbreviations:

A   Adkins, D. C., & Lyerly, S. B. *Factor analysis of reasoning tests.* Chapel Hill, N. C., University of North Carolina, 1951.

Cr   Christal, R. E. Factor analytic study of visual memory. *Psychological Monographs,* 1958, 7 (Whole No. 466).

ETS   Educational Testing Service, Princeton, N. J. *Kit of reference tests for cognitive factors,* by French, J. W., Ekstrom, Ruth B., & Price, L. A., 1963.

F   Fleishman, E. A., Roberts, M. M. & Friedman, M. P. A factor analysis of aptitude and proficiency measures in radiotelegraphy. *Journal of Applied Psychology,* 1958, 42, 129-137.

Kn   Karlin, J. E. A factorial study of auditory function. *Psychometrika,* 1942, 7, 251-279.

Ky   Kelley, H. P. Memory abilities: a factor analysis. *Psychometric Monographs,* No. 11, 1964.

LLT   Thurstone, L. L. A factorial study of perception. *Psychometric Monographs,* No. 4, 1944.

SPS   Sheridan Psychological Services, Box 837, Beverly Hills, California.

USAF   United States Air Force, Personnel Research Laboratory, Lackland Air Force Base, Texas. Forms modified in research at the University of Southern California are designated as USAF-M.

Cognition: The Figural Dimension

COGNITION OF FIGURAL UNITS—VISUAL (CFU—V) is the ability to recognize a figural entity, that is, to "close" figural information or perceive a complete visual form.

Tests

Gestalt Completion Test. Write the names of objects presented in silhouette figures with enough parts blotted out to make the task of cognition sufficiently difficult for testing purposes. (ETS) (34)*
Concealed Words Test. Recognize words in which part of each letter has been erased. (ETS) (34)
Peripheral Span. Recognize letters flashed 1/25th of a second in peripheral vision. Individually administered. (LLT)
Dark Adaptation. Recognize letters in dim illumination. Individually administered. (LLT)

A distinction must be made between factor tests for this ability and the tests which use amorphous stimuli (such as inkblots). In the factor tests, the known gestalt needs to be completed; in the inkblot and other tests similarly designed, there are many possible ways open to the subject for imposing his own gestalt upon the stimuli.

Few standardized educational tests tap this ability. Since so many students who have difficulty with learning to read also have trouble discriminating units, it would seem that this sort of task would be helpful for them. The publication, *Children's Highlights*, often has figural completion exercises which are presented as fun activities. Teachers may use these as models for seatwork in which they take from course-of-study materials the figural referents of reading words.

Speed-reading techniques often include tachistoscopic exercises similar to the factor tests in which the flashed stimuli range from incomplete figures (F) to numerals (S) and to words (M).

Curriculum Suggestions

This ability is often termed discrimination of units. Discrimination of units is a necessary ability for learning beginning reading and beginning arithmetic. The factor tests imply a "game" type of task. This can be profitably explored by the teacher who makes seatwork for her children. Especially useful are ditto masters for hand-drawn work. A seatwork game, using partial letters which are not yet well known, can serve as a readiness conditioning task for the child's learning the totality of the letter. Once the letters are completed by the student (using pencil), they can also be traced similarly as the teacher says the letter. An adaptation of the Fernald method of tracing sandpaper shapes is another suggestion.

This adaptation can also be used for remedial reading exercises where the concrete object and its label beneath are presented together and simultaneously with the object alone being partly obliterated so as to force closure by the student. Slides can also be made.

COGNITION OF FIGURAL UNITS—AUDITORY (CFU—A) is the ability to perceive auditory figural units (sounds) by organizing groups of successive inputs.

---

* See Legend for Factor Tests, for all such citations.

Tests

Dot Perception. Report how many dots, from 1 to 5, are given at the beginning or end of a series of code signals. (F)

Tests devised by Dorothea Paul (1964) for the Charles E. Merrill Publishing Company series, *Going Places,* offers one of the few series tests which stresses auditory cognition of sounds. Although the skills outlined are labeled with traditional educational terms, an analysis of the exercises and tests shows that they fall into very discrete factor-like categories such as CFU—V, CFU—A, CFC, NFC, EFU, and EFR—all of which are important in reading readiness. This series has been used successfully with children in educational therapy at the Los Angeles Child Achievement Center.

When students show difficulty in the attachment of phonic sounds to the visual representations, a model approach using auditory stimuli ought to be attempted to test for simple auditory cognition. Any method of enlisting auditory attendance or training auditory awareness can be used on a small group of children having such difficulties. Tape recorders with sounds of the tape where the pupil either repeats the sound patterns or writes them down will give training in auditory attending. The Bell and Howell Language Master offers great variety for use in these exercises.

The Seashore test of musical aptitude also tests auditory units as do some aspects of the Pintner-Patterson test involving the hitting of blocks for reproduction by the student of the sound patterns.

Curriculum Suggestions

The suggestions made for CFU—V may also be used for CFU—A if auditorially presented.

COGNITION OF FIGURAL CLASSES (CFC) is the ability to recognize classes of figural items of information.

Tests

Figure Classification. Recognize classes of three sets of figures each, then assign given figures to the classes. (39)
Picture Classification. Assign pictures to classes each defined by a group of three pictures. (35)
Figural Class Inclusion. Assign, from five alternatives, one figure that contains the same properties as two given figures. (39)

Aspects of this ability are frequently tested in reading-readiness tests such as the Vallet, Metropolitan, Frostig, ITPA, Binet, French, CTMM, and Lee-Clarke.

Curriculum Suggestions

The ability to classify is one which has great importance in concept formation and in "chunking" of bits of information for easier storage in memory. Too often it is assumed that the child can classify when he cannot, and classification tasks when used with young children having difficulty in language and reading skills have proved to be rewarding for both teacher and child. The task can be approached in several ways. If the child needs motoric experience, he can rifle through magazines and cut out his own pictures, paste them, and then classify them. The teacher may place pictures on cards (and thus control the subject matter according to the unit of study under way) and have the child impose his own classification scheme on it, or she can impose the classifications she wants him to come out with. It is a task which can be undertaken as an individual project. Periods of 20 minutes several times a week have improved reading skills in primary and high school students; attending has improved for some, and for others, hyperactivity has been lessened in the self-oriented activities stemming from classification.

There are several sources for getting small paper pictures: the dime store, magazines, trading cards. The student may collect them or the teacher may have them on hand. The child's task is simple:

1) Paste the pictures on 3 x 5 cards—child may cut them out if he needs to develop motor skills.

2) Put all the pictures that go together in one pile.

To develop cognition it is essential that the child impose his own classification scheme on the cards. He will have his own reasons. The task induces seeing details (units) and then seeing relations between them.

COGNITION OF FIGURAL RELATIONS (CFR) is the ability to recognize figural relations between forms.

Tests

Figure Analogies. From multiple choices, select a figure that completes an analogy. (11)

Figure Matrix. From multiple choices, select a figure to fill a matrix cell in a 3 x 3 matrix with a different relation in columns and rows. (34)

This ability, like CMU, vocabulary, is used extensively in intelligence testing. It generally falls under test sections called "non-verbal." Large portions of such tests which purport to measure intelligence because they correlate well with validated tests of intelligence are actually measuring only one ability. The Henman-Nelson uses this kind of item to a great extent. IQ scores which are permanently recorded as indices to general intelligence tests may be scores based on only one intellectual ability. The DAT devotes a subtest section to this ability; the CTMM also contains a similar subtest.

It is not that the tests are not reliably measuring what they purport to measure, but, rather, it is a question of the validity of the assumption that the obtained measure is a valid measure of intelligence. Thorndike defined intelligence primarily as a measure of the ability to see relations. In view of the SOI refinement of the concept of relations, we need to examine the issue of validity; we need to know with what the ability (or lack of it) to see relations is related. Which skills are predicated upon it? Which professions demand proficiency in seeing relations? What is the effect of relations on social adjustment, communications, academic success?

For several years the Miller Analogies Test, a test of relations, was depended upon as a selective criterion for graduate school admittance.

Many schools have either ceased using the Miller Analogies Test or, at least, have given it less weight in choosing graduate students. Scores on one test alone did not predict graduate success as well as had been expected. Again, the reason is obvious. The ability to cognize relations (any one ability), whether in figural, symbolic, or semantic dimensions, may neither be necessary nor sufficient for predicting graduate school success. As will be shown in SOI profiles (Chapter 11), gifted students may have strengths or weaknesses in the relations dimension, and their ability or lack of it seems to determine other kinds of behavior and interests than success in grades.

Curriculum Suggestions

Phonics Bingo, Lotto, and picture (figural) stimuli are tasks which are similarly related to the task demanded in the factor tests. Many components of subject matter can be used to develop matrices or row and column relationships. The units used are not so critical as is the task of recognizing the figural relations. (See Evaluation of Figural Relations.)

Although the differences between cognition of, evaluation of, and convergent production of figural relations will seem slight in actual practice, the differences are the same as differences between comprehending that these relations exist, making an evaluation or judgment about the correctness of the relations, or reproducing the next in a series.

COGNITION OF FIGURAL SYSTEMS (CFS) is the ability to comprehend arrangements and positions of visual objects in space.

Tests

Card Rotations Test.   From a group of six drawings of a card shown rotated and/or turned over, indicate which ones show the card not turned over. (ETS)

Cube Comparisons Test. Indicate which items present two drawings that can be of the same cube and which cannot, judging from the markings on the faces of the cubes. (ETS)

Guilford-Zimmerman Spatial Orientation.   Indicate the position of a boat with respect to the landscape after a pictured change in the boat's position. (SPS)

Tests of spatial orientation also appear in the DAT, in various industrial personnel-selection tests, in the CTMM, and in other group tests of reading readiness.

Curriculum Suggestions

This ability is not an easy one to adapt to schoolroom tasks. Whether or not tests of depth perception would actually factor on this ability is open to speculation. The classes in driver education do occasionally give exercises on depth perception of a type, and experts in the area generally find that boys do better on spatial orientation tasks than do girls. Perhaps it is that at an early age boys receive toys which depend on motor dexterity, and girls generally do not. If the teacher receives an SOI profile on a child who shows strengths in the figural dimension, she need not be too concerned about further tasks; if the student shows weaknesses in the figural dimension, then the determination about strengthening that disability will depend on considerations such as this: Should a weakness in semantics be taught through figural stimuli? Children who need to have kinesthetic experience precede abstract learning will benefit from tasks which teach him CFS. The Montessori philosophy stresses the importance of easy and frequent kinesthetic learning experiences.

We also need to ask: What future adult activities are most dependent on spatial orientation abilities? Certainly the arts (manual and esthetic), architecture, physics, vocational skills such as carpentering, dentistry, electronics, radio, woodwork, and even plastic surgery are all dependent on successful assimilation of skills such as spatial orientation and depth perception. A great many adults who are involved in such professions had to wait until high school to take vocational shops as electives.

COGNITION OF FIGURAL TRANSFORMATIONS (CFT) is the ability to visualize how a given figure or object will appear after given changes, such as unfolding or rotation.

Tests

Form Board Test. Indicate which scrambled pieces would fit together to form a given complete figure. (ETS)

Paper Folding Test. Select one of five drawings of fully-opened paper that shows how a given folded and punched paper would look unfolded. (ETS)

Surface Development Tests. Indicate which lettered edges in a drawing of a solid figure correspond to numbered edges, or dotted lines, in a plane diagram of the unfolded sides of the solid. (ETS)

Guilford-Zimmerman Spatial Visualization. Indicate among alternatives the position of an alarm clock after illustrated maneuvers. (SPS)

Two tests of this ability are found in the Stanford-Binet; one subtest is found in the WISC; the frequency is too limited to act as much more than a representative sampling of this ability.

One test which does test this ability was designed by Carl Hollow. It never reached great popularity but a limited amount of validation was made.

The Carl Hollow Square Scale Test consisted of layers of wood with oblique and acute angled sides which had to be fit together into a prespecified shape. This ability would seem to have importance for architects, structural engineers, finishing carpenters . . . , but figural abilities in general need to be explored. Their relationship to vocational tasks and the existence of sex differences need investigation.

Curriculum Suggestions

This ability may be difficult for primary teachers to attempt to use with their students. It is, of course, a prerequisite for success in mechanical drawing, physics, designing, and architecture. We do not know exactly how it is related to semantic tasks or what its importance is in the hierarchy of abilities, but we do know that many children who cannot learn abstract concepts which are visually presented can learn them when they are presented concretely in figural dimension. This approach to tasks is used successfully in Montessori schools and programs for the blind, culturally deprived, educationally handicapped, and neurologically impaired.

COGNITION OF FIGURAL IMPLICATIONS (CFI) is the ability to foresee the consequences involved in figural problems.

Tests

Competitive Planning. Starting with four incomplete, adjacent squares, add one line at a time, playing for two opponents, in such a way as to maximize the numbers of squares completed by both. (USAF-M) (10)
Route Planning. This is a maze-tracing test, in which the examinee indicates through which lettered points he must pass in order to reach the goal. (USAF-M) (10)
Planning a Circuit. Trace visually an electrical circuit diagram of overlapping wires and indicate which pair of terminals should be attached to a battery to make the circuit work. (USAF-M) (10)

Other tests such as paper folding, where the folds are indicated unseen, and variations on mazes, are frequently found in tests of intellectual ability. They appear in the Binet, WISC, Porteous Mazes tests, Nebraska Test of Learning Aptitude for Young Deaf Children developed by Hiskey (paper folding, completion of drawings), French's Pre-School Test, and Vallet's Test for Reading Readiness.

Curriculum Suggestions

Discussions with physics professors in several universities have pointed to the importance of this kind of ability for success in learning physics. Professor Patrick Taylor at the University of British Columbia described the ability in this way: "Although math is certainly important, it is not so necessary for success as is the ability to visualize figural objects graphically in third dimension. Some of this is memory, but for the most part the student must be able to conceptualize without the referent and particularly is this so in instances where the object or matter is entirely abstract."

We discussed at length the importance of play with concrete objects, of exposure to mechanical building toys and time to work with them imaginatively. One question which arose in discussions with other physicists was that of cultural expectations for boys as compared with girls. That is, girls are usually given dolls; boys are given tinkertoys. Would this have some bearing on the finding that few women enter or even take classes in physics? Such concerns lead to implications such as (1) relation of toys to later learning facility; (2) innate sex differences in abilities; (3) critical times for exposure to certain materials for best integration of any configuration of abilities.

The trend, re-occurring in education today, of giving more tactile experiences and manipulative materials for longer periods of time in the early grades would seem to indicate that educators are re-examining the importance of figural stimuli. This addition to curriculum is particularly helpful for children who have learning problems or who are essentially motor learners.

Specific suggestions for elementary and higher grades are difficult to make because there seems to be a period from third grade through seventh or eighth where the concentration in subject matter is in the visual, abstract, semantic, and symbolic subjects. When students, boys in particular, get into elective shops or mechanical drawing, they do become exposed to cognition and convergent production of figural items. Unless girls take home economics, art, or physics, they do not. Such helplessness in mechanical know-how may be fetching before the girl marries, but we who are predominantly semantic and abstractly oriented know how annoying and expensive it is if neither she nor her husband can solve problems involving figural content!

Cognition: The Symbolic Dimension*

COGNITION OF SYMBOLIC UNITS—VISUAL (CSU—V) is a visual ability to recognize graphic symbolic units such as words.

Tests

Word Combinations. Make a new word using the last letters of one word and the initial letters of the next word. (33)

Omelet Test. Recognize a word whose letters have been scrambled. (23)

---

* The reader who is interested in factor assessments of infant tests can find full descriptions in L. Stott & Rachel Stutsman Ball's "Infant and Preschool Mental Tests: Review and Evaluation," *SCRD* Monograph: Chicago, Serial No. 101, Vol. 30, No. 3, 1965.

Disemvoweled Words.   Recognize a word whose vowels have been removed. (38)

Correct Spelling.   Recognize whether or not given words are spelled correctly. (SPS) (38) This test is also found in the DAT, under spelling.

COGNITION OF SYMBOLIC UNITS—AUDITORY (CSU—A) is an auditory ability to decode auditory information in the form of language symbols.

Tests

Haphazard Speech.   Recognize short phrases spoken with unusual inflection and pitch changes. (Kn)

Illogical Grouping.   Recognize short phrases spoken with grouping contrary to sense of the passage. (Kn)

Singing.   Recognize words in a short selection sung with piano accompaniment. (Kn)

Curriculum Suggestions

Although the imaginative reader can think of many exercises which could be devised to teach this important cognition ability, it is apparent that none is commonly used. In fact, very few tests are available which do test for the ability. The appropriate place for developing such training exercises might well be in the language arts. Games can be developed and seatwork designed using the test descriptions as models. Individualized programs should be devised for differentiated individual SOI patterns found among students who have difficulty in attending, listening, auding, or monitoring teachers' auditory instruction.

Children with difficulties in reading endings can use training materials based on tasks for this ability. The scrambled letters for word lists are easily made up of words for spelling, reading, and social studies.

COGNITION OF SYMBOLIC CLASSES (CSC) is the ability to recognize common properties in sets of symbolic information.

Tests

Number-Group Naming.   State what it is that three given numbers have in common. (39)

Number Classification.   Select one of five alternative numbers to fit into each of four classes of three given numbers each. (39)

Best Number Pairs.   Choose one of three number pairs that makes the most exclusive (best) class. (33)

Other than the factor tests, few group-achievement tests include items in which symbols are classified.

Curriculum Suggestions

Using the above tests as models, teachers at any grade level can develop exercises within the context of their arithmetic tasks. Classifications in algebraic symbols will differ from classifications in multiplication or geometry. The primary goal would be the recognition of common properties in the subject matter. Chemistry, which is composed primarily of symbolic information, is predicated upon a classification model. Even here, though, the symbols can be classified in other unique ways. A close visual inspection of the meanings of the formulae for the purpose of other ways to classify them can actually reinforce and condition the expected learning.

COGNITION OF SYMBOLIC RELATIONS (CSR) is the ability to see relations between items of symbolic information.

Tests

Seeing Trends II. Find a repeated relationship between successive pairs of words in a series, the relations being in the form of spelling or alphabetical properties. (33)
Word Relations. This is a kind of analogies test in which the items of information related are words, the relations being in the form of spelling or alphabetical properties. (33)
The factor tests use analogical relations in a different manner from most tests; most often tests require understanding of the analogical relationships in meaning, quality, or use.
The Lorge-Thorndike intelligence tests for elementary schools incorporate a scattering of this kind of item. Generally, however, this specific task is seldom used.

Curriculum Suggestions

Since symbolic items are often numerical, and numerical items are not used in this factor, we can only speculate that the use of numerals for the devising of exercises to train this ability will in fact do so. If we ask the student to find relations between a list of odd numbers, or sets of odd numbers, we may actually be testing memory for symbolic relations, while the primary task is the cognition of those relations.

COGNITION OF SYMBOLIC SYSTEMS (CSS) is the ability to understand the systematic interrelatedness of symbols within an organized set.

Tests

Circle Reasoning. Discover the rule for marking one circle in sequence with other circles and with dashes. (33)

Letter Triangle.   Find the system by which letters of the alphabet are arranged in a triangular pattern with some vacant positions, then select one of five alternative answers (letters) to fill a designated position. (33)

Number Series.   Find the rule for series of numbers and write a description of each series. (11)

Letter Series.   Find the rule for series of letters and write the next two letters in each series. (11)

This kind of item is frequently found in culture-free tests such as Cattell's scale 2 — IPAT, the Army General Classification Test, parts of the Leiter Scale, and performance test sections which require understanding interrelatedness of numerals within a series.

Curriculum Suggestions

Variations of this particular task are so frequently found in tests that little explanation is necessary. However, tasks which might train this ability do need to be explained. That is, techniques for finding relatedness and rules on how to find the relatedness do need to be taught. At least, children ought to be exposed to these ways of looking at and analyzing the data on hand. Too often, the child is expected to generalize from his working knowledge to the comprehending of rules which may be involved in finding relationships between a series of numbers. It can be an enlightening experience for children when they receive blackboard instructions on a series and how it is related: Add 3 each time, or subtract 1 and 2 alternately, or add 3 and double the next number. When this is vocalized it soon dispels the mystery, mystique, and fear in numerical manipulations.

COGNITION OF SYMBOLIC IMPLICATIONS (CSI) is the ability to foresee or to be sensitive to consequences in a symbolic problem.

Tests

Word Patterns.   Arrange a given set of words efficiently in a kind of crossword-puzzle pattern. (33)

Symbol Grouping.   Rearrange scrambled symbols of three kinds to achieve a specified systematic order in as few moves as possible. (33)

S-Test.   Discover problems in items composed of numbers, letters, and words, and solve the problems. (33)

Achievement tests which include arithmetic reasoning problems also touch upon this ability.

Curriculum Suggestions

These kinds of abilities are typically taught and practiced in mathematics; what, perhaps, may not always be taught is the "talking out" or reasoning to arrive at implied solutions. Questions like: "What are the implied (and teacher needs to define 'implied') solutions of this statement? If you solve it in this manner, what will happen? If in this manner, then what?" Teachers know that questions such as these need to be taught individually, vocally, and visually and to the entire group so that those who rarely answer are required to answer. The additional teaching time may make a substantial improvement in students' future scores on tests involving numerical series.

Cognition: The Semantic Dimension

COGNITION OF SEMANTIC UNITS (CMU) is the ability to comprehend the meanings of words or ideas.

Tests

Guilford-Zimmerman Verbal Comprehension.   A multiple-choice vocabulary test (SPS) (39)
Reading Comprehension.   Answer multiple-choice questions concerning meanings in a paragraph. (USAF)
Information Test.   Part of the Wechsler Adult Intelligence Scale
Word Completion.   Write a synonym or short definition for each given word. (39)

This single cell tests the most familiar ability — the ability to comprehend the meanings of words, or vocabulary. Vocabulary appears on nearly every intelligence test. In many instances, although the items may be stated differently throughout the test, the correct answer is still a test of vocabulary. Since the onset of testing, vocabulary has played a major role in assessing intelligence. In fact, decisions about major life goals have often been based on test results for this one factor, CMU, vocabulary — decisions such as: college or not? first-or second-class standing for grouping? medicine or law? teaching or art? music or engineering? Almost every high-school counselor, psychologist, or college-entrance counselor has built into his own system of evaluation a place and a meaning for scores on vocabulary tests, and as a consequence, life decisions for counselees have been based on their performance in tests of this ability. Group achievement and intelligence tests still devote at least one-half of their items to this one ability. Yet we know today that there may be as many as 119 other abilities which also exist.

In almost every case, too, the score achieved by a student on one-half of any group test he takes is based more on whether he has seen or heard the word, not on whether or not he could comprehend it if he were exposed to it.

The gravest example of the directness of such limited evaluative use of test results is the sociological phenomenon known as "cultural deprivation." Educators who work in projects consistently report that, given the opportunity to hear words and learn what they mean, these "deprived" children are quite capable of increasing their vocabularies and thus attaining higher IQ scores.

Many urbanologists have stated publicly that a major solution to socio-economic problems in education lies, for example, in the bussing of deprived children to better schools. Psychologists, on the other hand, have found that those few who have been bussed may gain in social exposure, but they also take on a different set of problems. They are not a real part of the new environment, and they often lose touch with the old. No group of theoreticians can afford to see just one section of the system. The total involvement of the student with any of the problems he has in the system is a result of the individual's acting as a catalyst in his own life space. Thus, if vocabulary or exposure to vocabulary determines his IQ score or expected school achievement, then this suggests that the major solution is not only that he be bussed to a new environment, but rather that the deficits stemming from his immediate environment be attacked — that cognitive skills, which make foundations for learning, be defined and taught as subject matter in place of the traditional required course of study.

If it seems a long way from CMU to a solution for urban problems, then it should be remembered that the intent of the book is to look at the problems of individual exceptional students according to the components of their abilities. In a research study for a pilot program for Project Headstart (Meeker, 1965),* the students selected showed a normal population curve both on their Binet IQ's and on scores of ten Piaget tests. The resultant curves closely approximated each other. The surprising and outstanding finding was that higher scores were made by the older children (age range 3 to 4.11). That is, the best predictor of Binet IQ score and performance on the Piaget tests depended on age, whereas on the Brown-Berko word association test their responses in terms of normal linguistic expectancies showed no relationship between IQ and adequacy of linguistic ability. Thus, the major finding indicated that language and language usage were categorically deficient for this sample of culturally deprived children.

It is predictable that unless such children receive training in the use of their own language (English) their IQ's will continue to drop more and more below average as they progress in school. This latter occurrence is, of course, the situation frequently reported by investigators working with the phenomenon of cultural deprivation.

This pilot investigation pointed out that one cause for the continuation of depressed IQ scores was language usage and lack of familiarity with native syntax rather than low IQ scores — that lack of adequate vocabulary concepts dictated poor achievement in the schools.

The meaning is quite clear. In depressed areas, the curriculum for kindergarten and first grade should be concerned primarily with the use of vocal language and those vocabulary concepts on which learning depends.

---

* Unpublished study for Los Angeles City Schools, Division of Research.

COGNITION OF SEMANTIC CLASSES (CMC) is the ability to recognize common properties of words, ideas, and objects.

Tests

Word Classification. Select the one word in a set of four that does not belong to the class by virtue of its meaning. (39)
Verbal Classification. Assign each word to one of two classes, or to neither, each class being represented by a set of four words. (34)
Sentence Classification. Decide whether each given sentence conveys fact, possibility, or a name. (39)

Many of the exercises in *Creative Analysis** may be used both as tests of and training for this ability. Neither group achievement nor group intelligence tests approach semantic classification in this manner so it is not frequently experienced. Occasionally, in *Children's Highlights*, exercises of this kind are presented.

Curriculum Suggestions

Once semantic skills are developed to the point where seatwork can be devised to incorporate reading, the imaginative teacher will find several ways to explore this ability. Training for this skill occurs when the child is presented with lists of words and is asked to place all the words which are verbs in one list, the adjectives in another . . . . The primary teacher who concentrates on alphabetizing is also teaching classification. Some children who do classify well according to beginnings or endings, or who alphabetize correctly, cannot remember the ordering of letters within the alphabet itself. But, of course, the ordering of letters within the alphabet presents a system, and we know that working with a total system is predicated upon an ability other than simple classification. Ordering includes relations between the components within the system.

COGNITION OF SEMANTIC RELATIONS (CMR) is the ability to see relations between ideas or meanings of words.

Tests

Verbal Analogies I. From multiple choices select a word to complete a meaningful relationship. (34)
Word Matrix Test. Discover relations in rows and columns, then supply the missing word. (34)

This type of test item is well known as analogies, and so often occurs in intelligence tests that more explanation is unnecessary.

---

* Upton and Samson, *Creative Analysis* (New York: Dutton & Co., Inc., 1963).

Curriculum Suggestions

Students need exposure to and training in this kind of item before they are tested on analogies if a valid measure of power is expected. The importance of this ability lies more in the teaching of the skill rather than solely in the testing of it.

COGNITION OF SEMANTIC SYSTEMS (CMS) is the ability to comprehend relatively complex ideas.

Tests

Guilford-Zimmerman General Reasoning. A multiple-choice arithmetic-reasoning test in which numerical computation is minimized (SPS)
Ship Destination. Find the distance of a ship to a port, taking into account the influences of an increasing number of variables. (SPS) (39)
Necessary Arithmetical Operations. Given the facts of a problem, select from multiple choices the pair of number operations needed to solve the problem. (14)
Necessary Facts. Given all necessary facts but one, state the one that is missing to make the arithmetical problem structure complete. (31)
Problem Solving. Solve five-choice verbally stated problems, using arithmetic. (39)

Similar test items appear in the WISC and the Stanford-Binet as subtests. Within the general definition of the factor, most achievement tests include questions predicated on manipulating semantic translations of symbolic information. Items which are identical to the tests listed above, and those where a total paragraph is read (a system of ideas) demand that the student show comprehension of meaning derived from a system of words.

Curriculum Suggestions

This is a complex ability. The simplest approach would best be a setting up of a series of steps for solving certain problems involving their related parts the way Gallagher (1963, 1964) describes the analyses of the rudiments of solutions. The student must first observe a phenomenon; then to demonstrate that he comprehends it he must attempt to explain it — by ordering his thoughts into a systematic whole he arrives at the totality. It is questionable whether or not a large group can work on this kind of project. Small groups would allow maximum participation, and the challenge would probably be more successfully accepted by group members.

COGNITION OF SEMANTIC TRANSFORMATION (CMT) is the ability to see potential changes of interpretations of objects and situations.

Tests

Similarities. Give as many as six ways in which two given objects are alike. (32)

Social Institutions. Suggest two improvements each for institutions, such as taxes, divorce.... The score is the number of farsighted needed improvements given. (11)

Cartoons. Write as many as two "punch lines" for given cartoons. (11)

Some industrial tests use this kind of item but there are few, if any, educational tests which do. The ability to make transformations is generally considered to be creative because fluency of ideas in breaking sets is necessary.

Curriculum Suggestions

Using descriptions of the above tests as models, teachers can apply the same principles of learning to other subject matter. Some tasks can and should be auditory. Ways for transforming uses of objects or ideas should be expressed both in writing and in discussions. Suggested areas for assignments are:

History: What has made the mails and postal system "big business"? How can the costs of running the postal system be reduced?

Science: How many ways are electricity and levers alike?

Creative writing (after the students have seen a movie): Starting with the conflict in the story (explain), resolve the conflict before a crisis begins and show how the story would have ended. Example: In *Splendor in the Grass,* suppose the two sweethearts had married when they fell in love. How would the story have ended?

For younger children: Select a familiar story; point out where the story gets exciting because of the problem. (Brer Rabbit makes friends with Brer Fox.) Then how would the story have ended? Younger children should vocalize their endings when their writing skills are still slower than their vocal skills.

COGNITION OF SEMANTIC IMPLICATIONS (CMI) is the ability to anticipate or be sensitive to the needs of or the consequences of a given situation in meaningful terms.

Tests

Pertinent Questions. Write as many as four questions, the answers to which should help to reach a decision in a conflict situation. (SPS) (32)

Alternate Methods. List as many as six different ways of accomplishing a certain task. (10)

Seeing Problems.   Write as many as five problems arising from the presence of a given object. (35)
Apparatus Test.   Suggest two improvements in each of some common appliances. (32)

The nature of group intelligence test items is such that several answers are seldom possible. The Binet, however, does test this ability at some levels.

Curriculum Suggestions

Questions modeled after the test descriptions in language arts can be asked vocally or on paper. Exercises pertinent to the curriculum can be devised to be used as rainy-day games. Seatwork for language arts is an excellent way to introduce alternative solutions to conflicts. Games of this nature have been used experimentally with elementary and high-school students by Apt (1966). Recess and physical education periods provide good opportunities to explore games which solve current events or social problems.

Cognition: The Behavioral Dimension

COGNITION OF BEHAVIORAL UNITS (CBU) is the ability to understand units of expression, such as facial expression.

Tests

Faces.   Indicate which man's face expresses the same feeling or intention as a given woman's face. (34)
Expressions.   Indicate the gesture, posture, or expression that expresses the same thought, feeling, or intention as the given gesture, posture, or expression. (34)

Perhaps the closest any formal test items come in testing this ability are those few items found in the CTMM, Lee-Clarke, and the Binet, where the student is asked to choose which of four pictures is the prettiest or the best.

Curriculum Suggestions

Teachers can serve as excellent models for this kind of experience. Students may be asked to describe what the teacher is feeling by her facial expression. Students, too, can demonstrate while others, including teacher, guess. Most of us have witnessed how children can tell by the expression on a parent's face at the dinner table whether or not he must eat his vegetables before asking for dessert!

Perhaps it is those youngsters who cannot discriminate these nonverbal communications, or who cannot "read" gestures and expressions, who have social problems or develop them soon after their first group interactions in school.

COGNITION OF BEHAVIORAL CLASSES (CBC) is the ability to see similarity of behavioral information in different expressional modes.

Tests

Expression Grouping.   Choose the alternative expression that belongs with a given group of expressions. (SPS) (34)
Picture Exclusion.   Indicate the one photographed expression that does not belong with three other given photographed expressions on the basis of the thoughts, feelings, or intentions portrayed. (34)

Curriculum Suggestions

At the present time no such tasks are available. The teacher who wants to give pupils this kind of learning experience must use her own ingenuity to develop similar exercises.

COGNITION OF BEHAVIORAL RELATIONS (CBR) is the ability to understand social relationships.

Tests

Social Relations.   Select one of three given statements that expresses the feeling of a given face, taking into account the relationship demonstrated in another, interacting, face. (34)
Silhouette Relations.   Select one of three photographed faces that expresses the individual's feeling or intention in a silhouette relationship between two people. (34)

Curriculum Suggestions

The "funnies" and cartoons capitalize on this ability. The popularity of comics is dependent on two things: the reader's free use of imagination to conjure up the meanings, and the relief they provide the reader from visual-verbal work. Remedial reading teachers have long recognized the value of comic books for putting a positive value on words and for developing goal-acceptance among their pupils. Teachers generally can choose comic books to show and discuss with pupils how to "read" facial expressions.

COGNITION OF BEHAVIORAL SYSTEMS (CBS) is the ability to comprehend a social situation or sequence of social events.

Tests

Missing Pictures.   Select one of three photographed social interactions that completes a given story, making sense of the thoughts and feelings of the actors in the photographed story. (SPS) (38)

Missing Cartoons.   Select one of four alternative cartoons that completes a cartoon strip, making sense of the thoughts and feelings of the characters. (SPS) (38)

Although the Healy Picture Completion Tests show total scenes where humans are involved in activities, the task of supplying the correct part which is missing does not necessarily involve sequencing. This early test was subsequently incorporated into the Pintner-Patterson Performance Scale, and tests similar to it were used by Wechsler for the WISC and WAIS. However, the exact task required of the subject on these tests differs from that required on factor tests where the subject is required to order the pictures temporally in terms of occurrence.

Curriculum Suggestions

It would seem that this ability is fundamental to good social functioning, social adjustment, and comprehending social expectations. As SOI analyses now stand, neither the Binet nor the WISC give verified information in individual profiles about deficits in this area, so the usefulness of materials devised to teach this ability has to be speculative; that is, if a child has social problems perhaps it is because he is unable to read his environment correctly. The validation of such relationships is currently under investigation. The teacher's recourse here, unless she is an artist, is to use comic strips which apply to unique situations.

COGNITION OF BEHAVIORAL TRANSFORMATION (CBT) is the ability to reinterpret either a gesture, a facial expression, a statement, or a whole social situation so that its behavioral significance is changed.

Tests

Picture Exchange.   Select one of three alternative photographs that, when substituted for a given picture in a story sequence, will change the meaning of the story by altering the thoughts, feelings, or intentions of the actors. (SPS) (34)

Social Translations.   Select one of three diadic pairs between which a given verbal statement would have a different meaning or intention from that given. (SPS) (34)

Other tests of this ability are not commonly found in group tests, although the Davis-Eells Games, Verbal Problems, may touch upon the ability.

Curriculum Suggestions

The factor test descriptions may be used as models by teachers and counselors for organizing special periods devoted to Behavioral Training.

COGNITION OF BEHAVIORAL IMPLICATIONS (CBI) is the ability to draw implications or make predictions about what will happen following a given social situation.

Tests

Cartoon Predictions. Select one of three cartoon situations that can be predicted from the given cartoon, based on the feelings and intentions of the cartoon characters. (34)

There are tests which are similar to (but not exactly like) the factor tests described, in which cartoons are used to describe situations where tasks required of the examinee differ.

Curriculum Suggestions

Here again, the teacher would have to search for and select those cartoons which would help her get across the material she needs to teach. She could, of course, explain the task to her students and have them search and select cartoons for homework. This might be particularly helpful for those students who need aid in understanding social situations and correct social reactions.

FIGURE 4-1
FACTORS IDENTIFIED IN MEMORY

	Figural	Symbolic	seMantic	Behavioral
Units	MFU (I) *	MSU	MMU	
Classes	(I)	MSC	MMC	
Relations	(I)	MSR	MMR	
Systems	MFS V MFS A (I)	MSS	MMS	
Transformations	(I)	MST	MMT	
Implications	(I)	MSI	MMI	

*Currently being investigated

50

4

Memory Factors

Memory: The Figural Dimension

MEMORY FOR FIGURAL UNITS (MFU) is the ability to remember given figural objects.

Tests

Reproduction of Designs.   Reproduce geometric-type designs having had a brief exposure to them. (Ky)
Map Memory.   Select from multiple choices the segment of a map previously studied. (USAF)
    The Binet, Memory for Visual Figures Test, and the French tests have items predicated upon this ability. The Bender-Gestalt may be used as a memory test for older children, as may the Winterhaven for children under eight.

Curriculum Suggestions

    When memory for discrimination of figural units is found to represent a disability, this student will often have difficulty in learning word attack skills, phonics, and other rudiments of reading. Task practice will establish a longer span and accuracy of reproduction. Use of the Language Master is suggested. It allows the child to see the card with the stimulus figure on it, hear it, and at the same time hold the task in mind while he goes to a blackboard to reproduce it. Thus, three sensory modes are practiced. The length of time between hearing and seeing the figure can be extended for the student by counting so many seconds before reproducing the figure on the board, on paper, or in another room. The task can be expanded to include phonics, letters, numerals (Symbols—MSU), as well as words and phrases later on (seMantics—MMU).

Hiding objects or pictures of objects is also another game-like task which can be employed to build this ability. The well-known shell game (a small object under a walnut shell) is a similar activity. In most instances, this simple ability must be trained on an individual or small group basis.

MEMORY FOR A FIGURAL SYSTEM—VISUAL (MFS—V) is the ability to remember the spatial order or placement of given visual information.

Tests

Space Memory.   Identify the form that was previously exposed in each of five sections within five squares. (Cr)
Position Memory.   Recall the position of a number-word pair approximately four hours after the initial administration of the Number-Word test. (Ky)

Spatial orientation and non-language tests in the California Test of Mental Maturity (CTMM) would be testing this ability if they were used as memory tests. Again, the memory requirement is not, however, a part of the test (see CFR, EFR, and NFR) and would have to be added as an extra task before these group tests were clearly testing memory.

Curriculum Suggestions

The Position Memory factor test description will serve as a model for imposing an additional requirement on any material used. For example, given seatwork to take home, the child may not only have to answer questions about the seatwork, but the next day, after the work is turned in, he may be asked to indicate where a certain item was on the paper he took home.

This is exactly the task required in chemistry for learning the positions of elements. The visual-minded student will have an easier time recalling the elements than will the auditory or motor learner; nevertheless, tasks pointed toward training visual position memory as exercised above may facilitate this ability for students who are not inclined towards visual memory.

MEMORY FOR A FIGURAL SYSTEM—AUDITORY (MFS—A) is the ability to remember auditory complexes of rhythm or melody.

Tests

Musical Memory.   Recognize musical compositions heard earlier. (Kn)
Rhythm.   Recognize patterns of the tape. (Kn)

The Knox Blocks Test does test this ability and includes memory span as a component in the recall of pattern. The Seashore Music Test also gives measurements on MFS—A.

Curriculum Suggestions

Teaching for figural systems on an auditory input is not necessarily related to music, although music offers a rich source of ideas. Rattles of different pitches and sounds, weights and surfaces which vary in texture, all offer avenues of kinesthetic figural training. The class can, as a group, listen to rhythms of well-known songs and try to identify them. They, or the teachers, can use either their feet or hands to tap out familiar rhythms. Lengths of sounds (whole note, half notes) can be taught and practiced with instruments or voice tones; students can be asked to recall the order of presentation for repetition. A program for teaching piano and music to blind children was developed by Lenore McGuire whose approach depends on and trains MFS.

Memory: *The Symbolic Dimension*

MEMORY FOR SYMBOLIC UNITS (MSU) is the ability to remember isolated items of symbolic information, such as syllables and words.

Tests

Memory for Listed Nonsense Words. Recognize whether or not given nonsense syllables were on a previously studied page. (38)
Memory for Nonsense Words—Free Recall. Recall three-letter nonsense words presented on a previously studied page. (38)
Memory for Digital Units. Recognize whether or not given two-digit numbers were previously read aloud. (38)

Pure memory of this short-span type is rarely tested in group tests. Those group tests which include items such as "Put a mark on the picture that shows the most birds eating" are most likely testing cognition, whereas group test items which show a picture and then have the student recall what items were pictured are testing figural and symbolic memory.

Curriculum Suggestions

This particular ability can be taught quite readily with the material at hand in math workbooks or spelling books by the teacher's suggesting that the child turn the book over and recall how many of something there were on the page. As the factor tests above indicate, the page should be studied for a given amount of time with the task in mind. Pictures cut from magazines which contain numerals can be used for study and recall by small groups and by the whole class. Students can cut and paste their own memory pictures using stimuli taken from required subject matter; for example: "How many 2's were there on the page?" "How many a's were there?" Given a page of numerals or letters, "circle (point to or write which numerals (or letters) you see on this page which were on the page you just studied."

Older students may be equally in need of similar exercising. It should be emphasized that it is not the content of the material that is important so much as it is the task required; i.e., memory.

MEMORY FOR SYMBOLIC CLASSES (MSC) is the ability to remember symbolic class properties.

Tests

Memory for Number Classes — Recall. Recall the class properties of groups of three numbers each that were studied on a previous page. (38)
Memory for Nonsense Word Classes. Indicate which of four nonsense words given in each item on a test page represent a class given on a previously studied page. (39)
Memory for Word Classes. Indicate whether each of a number of words on a test page represents a class studied on a previous page. (39)

Curriculum Suggestions

Before expecting students to be able to carry out tasks of this nature, the teacher should spend some time teaching the concept of classification. Both the concept and the vocabulary she uses may be confusing to the child until each has been explained and examples given. Those students who have no difficulty with the concept can be helpful as partners for those who do have difficulty, and students who show no comprehension of the concept at all will, of course, need individual help.

The concept of classification is an important one and is one which is almost foundational to much of the subject matter the child is expected to learn. The factor test descriptions may be used as models. Perhaps more simple tasks will involve the children's imposing their own classification systems on numerals and letters at hand, first, and then using these as study pages.

MEMORY FOR SYMBOLIC RELATIONS (MSR) is the ability to remember definitive connections between units of symbolic information.

Tests

Memory for Word-Number Relations. Remember the connections, based on symbolic properties, between words and numbers given in two pairs and then indicate which number from four alternatives is associated with a new word on the basis of the remembered connection. (38)

Memory for Name Relations.   Remember what kind of last name goes with first names, based on symbolic properties, and on the basis of memory choose one last name from four alternatives that goes with a given new first name. (38)

Memory for Letter Series.   Recognize the series rule associated with a given letter on a previously studied page. (38)

Memory for Numerical Relations.   Recall the symbolic relationship between numbers presented in pairs on a previously studied page. (38)

Most tests which include symbolic relations items require that the student find the relationship already involved. (See CSR and NSR.) In memory tasks, the relationships need to be studied first and then given separately for recall.

Curriculum Suggestions

We all know how much difficulty some of us have in recalling names of people we have met. And even though we, as adults, can smile at our own human failing, we may not, nevertheless, appreciate that for the child who does not have the confidence which comes with knowing about universal human failings, the inability to remember is often so frightening that it threatens the establishing of a good academic self-concept. Children need to be taught relations first; they need to have time in school to study what they have learned; and then, they need to be given time for recall with additional time to check their corrections.

Each factor-test description can serve as a model for various kinds of activities to develop for children. Practice and mnemonic cues need to be given specifically and even intensely to develop this ability. A suggested time allotment for younger children is: ten minutes to go over and discuss the relationships, ten minutes to study them, a break for recess, ten minutes to reproduce the studied relationships, and five minutes to check their results. Each child can keep his own score so that he is competing with his own memory span to increase it. Understanding one's progress and making a graph of one's own scores are good evaluation techniques. Here the student learns to graph data while his competition is with himself and his rewards are immediately self-evident.

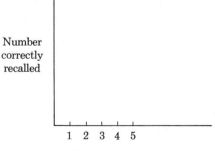

Days of study — Tom

MEMORY FOR A SYMBOLIC SYSTEM (MSS) is the ability to remember the order of symbolic information.

Tests

Memory for Transpositions.   Recognize changes in two auditory presentations in the order of two sets of four numbers each.   (38)
Consonant, Digit, and Nonsense Word Span. Recall series of consonants, digits, and nonsense words in order after auditory or visual presentation. (38)
Memory for Order of Listed Numbers.   Recognize which of four alternative numbers was presented first in a list of twelve numbers on a previously studied page.

The Seashore Music Test requires an ability of this kind for successful scores in timing and other musical components.

Experiments in nonsense syllables and paired-associate learning test this kind of ability when memory spans are tested. Group tests given in schools do not usually include such tasks, but the WISC, Binet, ITPA, and other individual tests which test backwards digit spans do test this ability in immediate memory.

Curriculum Suggestions

Descriptions of the factor tests will serve as models in which phonetics, arithmetic combinations, and misspelled words are used. Students need training in this ability if their spans are short. A general weakness in immediate auditory memory span is often the cause of poor achievement in students with good IQ's. Although backward span for numerals does factor separately from forward span for semantics, generalization often spreads to auditory stimuli. Thus, if the teacher depends heavily on vocal direction for tasks, her efforts in explaining may not be assimilated by those students with poor memory spans.

An individual exercise for those children suspected of having short memory spans is this: Digits should be presented vocally or visually on separate 3 x 5 cards on Language Master tape cards, or slides. The latter is a basic exercise for speed reading and has had favorable results there as well as in Educationally Handicapped classes. The student need only write down the span from memory after exposure. Twenty-minute periods, twice a week, of immediate memory training is recommended for students who show deficits in MSU, MSS, MMU, and MMS.

MEMORY FOR SYMBOLIC TRANSFORMATIONS (MST) is the ability to remember changes in symbolic information.

Tests

Memory for Word Transformations Recognize which of two divisions of a large word into two smaller words is the same as that presented on a previously studied page. (38)

Memory for Hidden Transformations. Recognize whether or not words hidden in sentences are formed in the same way they were formed on a previously studied page. (38)

When words are taken out of contextual meaning and used unmeaningfully, they can be regarded as symbols. Occasionally *Children's Highlights* has tasks which tap this ability. Other tests of this kind have been devised by investigators working in the area of creativity. Private industry employs such tests when interviewing for creative personnel.

Curriculum Suggestions

A double purpose can be served by using exercises to train this ability: memory is worked on, and at the same time, creativity is explored. The tests may come out of the materials at hand for the class. If, for example, the study page holds sentences and directions stating "The name of what object is hidden in each of these sentences?" and the object always occurs as part of a compound word, the student will expect to underscore only the object in a compound word: "He made a snow*ball*." Or combined beginnings and endings may be used: "Keep a ta*b all* the time, or you might forget." Either version could be used to break sets of expectancies.

MEMORY FOR SYMBOLIC IMPLICATIONS (MSI) is the ability to remember arbitrary connections between symbols.

Tests

Guilford-Zimmerman Numerical Operations. Add, subtract, multiply, and divide numbers—a multiple-choice test. (SPS) (33)

Number-Letter Association. Recall letters arbitrarily associated with numbers upon presentation of the number. (38)

Addition Test. Add sets of one- and two-digit numbers. (ETS)

Division Test. Divide two- and three-digit numbers by single digits. (ETS)

Subtraction and Multiplication Test. Subtract two-digit numbers; multiply two-digit numbers by single digits. (ETS)

Tests for this ability are almost as universally a part of academic tests as are tests for vocabulary (CMU).

Curriculum Suggestions

Curriculum suggestions need not be made here, since teachers are most familiar with training in this area.

Memory: The Semantic Dimension

MEMORY FOR A SEMANTIC UNIT (MMU) is the ability to remember isolated ideas or word meanings.

Tests

Picture Memory.   Recall names of common objects pictured on a previously studied page. (37)
Recalled Words.   Recall words presented on a previously studied page. (37)
    This type of test does appear occasionally in reading-readiness tests but not solely as a memory test; rather, it contributes to a composite score.

Curriculum Suggestions

    This ability may be strengthened by using exercises similar to those suggested for MSU and is easily adapted for primary grades. Pictures identical to those used in word charts and pre-primers are reinforcing for reading. These kinds of exercises are recommended as seatwork and as slides for all beginners and later for slower learners or students who need to drop down to a lower experimental level. As an adjunct to the task, students may be asked to search for and cut out pictures to go with words in their word box.

MEMORY FOR SEMANTIC CLASSES (MMC) is the ability to remember verbal or ideational class properties.

Tests

Classified Information.   Recognize classes similar to those given on a previously studied page. (39)
Picture Class Memory.   Indicate whether or not a given two-element class represents the same concept as one given on a previously studied page. (39)

Curriculum Suggestions

    Test *one* in the non-language section of the CTMM series tests this particular ability. It is a test of auditory memory for semantic classes, and even though scores on it may be penalizing to the student who is primarily a visual learner, or to the child who has poor auditory memory, it is, nevertheless, one of the few group tests which gives a measure of auditory memory for semantic classes.
    Teachers can adapt materials for this ability from any course of study materials. What is important is that when the material is used for a memory task, it must be presented either visually (separately) or auditorially. Thus students will be given practice and training in both modal memory abilities.

MEMORY FOR SEMANTIC RELATIONS (MMR) is the ability to remember meaningful connections between items of verbal information.

Tests

Remembered Relations. Complete sentences from alternatives in a manner consistent with previously studied relationships. (37)
Recalled Analogies. Recall missing elements for previously studied incomplete verbal analogies. (37)

Finding seMantic relations is a familiar task, but it is rarely used as a memory test covering material immediately after study.

Curriculum Suggestions

Analogies and other relations should be presented as part of the course of study in English and Language Arts. So often, however, what happens is that the student is suddenly confronted with such items for the first time on a test. The simplest way to approach memory for relations between semantics is to give a page of analogies with all parts left in. The student studies them at school or home and then is given the test covering those specific analogies. His task later is to supply the missing part, which may occur any place in the structured analogy.

Again, visual as well as auditory exercises should be given to train this ability.

MEMORY FOR A SEMANTIC SYSTEM (MMS) is the ability to remember meaningfully ordered verbal information.

Tests

Learned Information. Reproduce a short essay, with ideas in proper sequence, given several key terms in scrambled order. (37)
Memory for Test Order. Indicate whether or not a given test preceded another in a test booklet just completed. (37)

The Stanford-Binet and the WISC tap this ability, as do many of the remedial reading tests.

Curriculum Suggestions

Words in sentences can be read to students with key words given to them visually. The words are to be placed in correct order as previously read. This exercise can be performed visually, or vocally. The input can be visual with the output vocal, or the input can be given vocally with auditory reception and motoric output. The mode of input and output should be varied for the entire group and, of course, should be stressed according to individual needs for small groups when those needs have been identified.

If complexity is desired, sentences can be stretched into paragraphs. Children who have shown weaknesses on the ITPA in Association and Sequencing will need tasks of this nature if their weaknesses are to be strengthened.

MEMORY FOR SEMANTIC TRANSFORMATIONS (MMT) is the ability to remember changes in meaning or redefinitions.

Tests

Double Meanings. Recognize pairs of definitions that were not presented as words with double meanings in sentences previously studied. (37)
Homonyms. Recognize a definition that matches the definition of the "other element" in a pair of previously studied homonyms. (37)

Except for teacher-made tests, it is not likely that commercial tests would be available to fit this cell; the task does require previous study.

Curriculum Suggestions

Spelling lists for the semester can be reorganized so that there is a pairing of homonyms and/or synonyms which can be presented for study in the manner described by the factor tests.

Vocabulary can be treated in the same manner and taught as a separate part of the language arts program on a regular basis. Too often we depend on homework practice to develop memory; but, if we are to train for semantic transformation, the transformation of the original material ought to be more closely tied in time to the changed material. Such an approach makes the task one of short-term memory rather than one of long-term or stored, well-practiced memory. The debate continues between theorists on whether the former leads to or develops into the latter. For the teacher's purposes, a short-term approach is probably easier to administer and allows for more frequent evaluations of progress.

MEMORY FOR SEMANTIC IMPLICATIONS (MMI) is the ability to remember arbitrary connections between pairs of meaningful elements of information.

Tests

Related Alternatives. Recognize objects that are related to persons' jobs, based on studying a page of name-job pairs. (37)
Books and Authors. Recall probable occupations for given fictitious persons after studying a page of name-book pairs. (37)

Paired Associates Recall. Recall word-word paired associates. (38)

Most mechanical tests include items similar to those found in *Related Alternatives*. A new test for the purpose of vocational selection has been developed for illiterates and bilinguals. Hunt and Benoit (1967), using funds from the Bureau of Public Assistance, were given instructions to develop an interest test which avoided test anxiety and negated reading and writing skills. It was hoped that a means of exposing illiterates to vocations in order to find out which jobs might interest them could be developed. These men were on welfare but they sincerely wanted to work. Companies and other places of employment that hired unskilled laborers were visited by the authors. Pictures were taken of tools and of people using the tools at work. Slides were made and then shown to the men on welfare. Automotive and manufacturing scenes were stressed. The resulting test,* though experimental, proved successful. The men were able to choose vocations of interest to them. The test is called HABIT (Hunt and Benoit Interest Test).

Similar tests for educable mental retardates at the high-school level should be developed since vocational training for this sample of students needs similar serious consideration.

Curriculum Suggestions

Imaginative use of subject matters can be attempted in much the same manner as explored by Hunt and Benoit. Training for implications requires teaching at an abstract, non-referent level, and it is expected that memory for previously taught implications will result. *Books and Authors* is a most promising model to follow as a guideline.

---

* Information about the test is on file with the Bureau of Public Assistance, Los Angeles.

FIGURE 5-1
FACTORS IDENTIFIED IN EVALUATION

	Figural	Symbolic	seMantic	Behavioral
Units	EFU (I)*	ESU	EMU	
Classes	(I)	ESC	EMC	
Relations	(I)	ESR	EMR	
Systems	(I)	ESS	EMS	
Transformations	(I)	EST	EMT	
Implications	(I)	ESI	EMI	

*Currently being investigated

5

Evaluation Factors

Evaluation: The Figural Dimension

EVALUATION OF A FIGURAL UNIT (EFU) is defined as the ability to judge units of figural information as being similar or different. Judgments are based on minor aspects of the information. (In the figural column [FIG. 5-1] there is only one clearly identified cell—EFU.)

Tests

Guilford-Zimmerman Perceptual Speed. Identify among five similar ones the drawing of a common object that is identical with the given object. (SPS) (33)
Identical Forms. Mark all forms in a row that are identical with the one at the left of the row. (LLT) (33)
   This item is frequently encountered in reading-readiness tests where the child is asked to mark all those figures or forms in one row that are identical with those of a model (usually placed at the left).

Curriculum Suggestions

   Primary teachers will recognize EFU types of items in the reading-readiness and reading-achievement tests they administer. A child's ability to discriminate units (cognition) and determine their similarities and differences has proved to be vital for success in learning to read. Exercises using these tests as models may give impetus to developing reading skills.
   Although the remaining figural cells are still being inves-

tigated, it is possible to conceptualize them. One purpose for which the model may be used is prediction. That the tests as yet do not factor separately might well be due to the possibility that composite abilities are being tested.

The last five abilities are under investigation; therefore their descriptions here are speculative. Although the abilities can be defined, the actual testing for them as speculations would probably find evaluative and convergent-production factors involved in the performance and demonstration of the factors.

Evaluation of Figural Products Still Under Investigation

EVALUATION OF FIGURAL CLASSES (EFC) would define an ability to classify units specified in some way. The task for the student would be to analyze how they are classified and then judge how other units are similarly classified in another group of figures or forms.

EVALUATION OF FIGURAL RELATIONS (EFR) between groups of figures would seem to describe a task frequently found in many tests of mental maturity, such as the CTMM, Henman-Nelson, reading-readiness tests, and others where there is a progressive change in lines in a sequence of forms or figures, and where the student is to choose the next form to follow based on his evaluation of what the relations are between the figures or forms in the sequence.

EVALUATION OF A FIGURAL SYSTEM (EFS) would seem to define, in part, an ability to evaluate a system of figural units which have been grouped in some manner. The evaluation would depend on prespecified requirements. For example, in the Binet blocks tower building and comparison of balls tasks, and in the Gesell Developmental Tests (Stott and Ball, 1963), the task cannot be completed until the child has made an accurate judgment about the composites of the system he is asked to reproduce.

EVALUATION OF A FIGURAL TRANSFORMATION (EFT) is difficult to conceptualize. Perhaps the presentation of a series of figures which are different perspectives of the model might conceptually fill this cell, if the student is asked to choose the same figure from the alternative; however, this closely parallels spatial orientation tests.

EVALUATION OF FIGURAL IMPLICATIONS (EFI) might be defined as the ability to evaluate the adequacy or consistency of implied lines to complete a given form from a series presented.

Evaluation: The Symbolic Dimension

EVALUATION OF SYMBOLIC UNITS (ESU) is the ability to make rapid decisions regarding the identification of letter or number sets.

Tests

Symbol Identities. Judge whether both members of pairs of words and numbers are the same or different. (SPS) (33)

Letter "U." Check all words in long lists that contain the letter "U." (33)

First Digit Cancellation. In a row of 30 digits, indicate each digit that is like the first one in the row. (ETS)

Other tests of this ability are those which measure clerical speed and accuracy, such as is found in the DAT and the Minnesota Clerical Test.

Curriculum Suggestions

Many teachers use exercises of this type in language arts seatwork; e.g., Make an *S* if they are the same and a *D* if they are different.

$$489 \qquad 498$$

$$\text{cram} \qquad \text{cram}$$

EVALUATION OF SYMBOLIC CLASSES (ESC) is the ability to judge applicability of class properties of symbolic information, that is, judging of a class in which to place numbers, letters, or signs.

Tests

Best Number Class. Decide in which class a given number belongs so as to receive the most possible points. The classes and their points are: EVEN MULTIPLES—1 point; ODD MULTIPLES—2 points; SQUARES —3 points; PRIMES—4 points. (33)

Sign Changes II. Choose the sign changes that make the expression into correct equations (formerly recommended for ESR). (33)

Curriculum Suggestions

At the primary level in teaching beginning arithmetic, students might be presented with a sheet of numerals and asked to choose which of many numerals could be placed in the "even numbers" class, which in the "odd numbers" class, or which in the "tens" or "twenties" class. The purpose is to teach a concept or a "bit" of knowledge which identifies a numeral with one class. One might also want to teach understanding relations between members of any class. This will require demonstrating the processes which the teacher goes through step by step as she makes the evaluations for the students; i.e., verbally "walking through" her thinking openly.

EVALUATION OF SYMBOLIC RELATIONS (ESR) is the ability to make choices among symbolic relationships of similarity and consistency in given letters or numerals.

Tests

Symbol Manipulation.   Judge whether symbolic conclusions based on given premises are true or false. (33)
Related Words I.   Choose the alternative word pair with a relation most like that of the given pair. (33)

Curriculum Suggestions

Similar exercises can be used to teach letter relationships as, for example, in the teaching of phonetics. The beginning reading process depends primarily on the child's ability to discriminate, establish, and maintain symbolic relationships between discrete units. Boardwork emphasizing the auditory aspects of relationships should be supplemented with seatwork emphasizing the visual aspects of relationships, and in both instances each individual student should participate. This is time consuming at first, but it serves as a personalized reinforcement each time the student participates or watches. Many neurologically impaired children cannot learn isolated phonetic sounds so long as the symbolic and semantic relationships remain unrelated. This inability is a common problem among children referred to remedial reading clinics. Phonetic sounds must be tied to the semantics before the children make progress. On the other hand, there are children who can learn the symbolic aspects of language but who have great difficulty with the semantic aspects and must have the symbolic tied to the figural. The teacher who finds one of her pupils able to do one kind of task but not the other is aware that symbolic and semantic tasks are not necessarily related for some children. Fortunately, most children will eventually make necessary associations between the symbolic and the semantic aspects of language; however, when a reading disability can be traced to the child's inability to attach the semantic representations to figural or symbolic referents, then these exercises need to be given specifically.

The Gillingham and Stillman (1960) method for teaching reading is one which has often proved successful with this type of student when others have failed. In their method, the relations between sound and symbol associations must be established first, and the gradual conditioning of symbolics to semantics takes place through rigorous training.

EVALUATION OF SYMBOLIC SYSTEMS (ESS) is the ability to estimate appropriateness of aspects of a symbolic system.

Tests

Way-Out Numbers.   Choose the one alternative number from a list of four ordered numbers that is farthest away from the other three. (33)
Series Relations.   Choose one of the three arithmetic operations that best relates each number in a given series to the previous number. (33)

Curriculum Suggestions

Children are rarely given answers to problems or allowed to solve them by making evaluations of possible solutions. The new-math series (SRA), however, does occasionally include similar opportunities to perform this task in some parts of the workbooks. For the most part, seatwork to strengthen this ability has to be made by the teacher. Examples include:

VOWELS

a   i   w   y   e   u   l   Which letters go
together?   Why?

CONSONANTS

a   l   o   s   p   x   z   b   Which letters go
together?   Why?

NUMERALS

159   862   117   133   175   Which number does
not belong?   Why?

If examples appear on one sheet, there should be at least two lines left for the student to indicate his reasons.

In order for a child to be able to evaluate a system, the components of that system need to be clearly identifiable. As the student becomes familiar with looking at the totality of a system, he may not necessarily have to identify the components in a separate process, and, of course, there are students who do seem to "know"—who take in large gulps of information as though they were bits.

Children whose Binets have shown strength in the *Systems Dimension in Evaluation* are invariably the "organizers." As one teacher reported, "He approaches the task, new and unfamiliar to him, along with the other students, and, while others are still appraising the situation, he not only has a solution for it, he already knows who in the group can do what job best."

This anecdote does not imply a "systems" kind of personality (efficiency experts, trouble shooters, research-ideas men), although there may be such, given training and opportunity. Its purpose is to alert the teacher to watch for pupils who, showing facility in such tasks, can be given additional opportunities for growth.

EVALUATION OF SYMBOLIC TRANSFORMATIONS (EST) is the ability to judge whether or not an ordering of substitutive symbols is adequate.

Tests

Jumbled Words. Judge whether or not words could be made by mixing the letters of a given word. (33)

Curriculum Suggestions

Children are familiar with contests in which the requirement for winning is based on the most words which can be made from the letters in a given word. This type of task can also be used in primary grades in the teaching of spelling where students can be asked to generate other words from a master list. This assignment can be approached visually, and a type of conditioning for spelling the original word correctly occurs each time the student studies the master word in order to form other words from it. It can also be approached auditorially. That is, the master word (a familiar one) is spelled aloud and the students must keep in mind all the letters as they vocalize the small words they form. The auditory-vocal exercise is more difficult, of course, since students have no visual cues and must draw from memory. They insert letters not in the word and need frequent repetition of the spelling of the master word. Memory and evaluation operations are involved here. Sound-alike words can be verbalized in this manner too.

A similar approach to arithmetic may be used: The pupil is given a numeral from which he is to extract as many addition or subtraction facts as he can. By fourth grade, multiplication and division facts can also be included.

EVALUATION OF SYMBOLIC IMPLICATIONS (ESI) describes the ability to judge whether there is consistency of, probability of, or inferences from given symbolic information.

Tests

Abbreviations.   Choose one of three alternative words that a given abbreviation best implies. (33)

The letters, presented in a heretofore unused combination, imply a known word either by similarity of appearance or sound.

Curriculum Suggestions

The following mathematical task is a hypothesized one to fulfill requirements of the definition:

Given a series of addition (subtraction, multiplication, or division) facts, request the student to choose (from a series of stated verbal descriptions) that series which best implies the procedure for solution that fits the given fact. For example, on the left side of the page may appear the numerals $4 + 3 + 1 = 8$. On the right side of the page appear several written problems, some of which eventuate in a different total and one of which may or may not be correct. For example: A boy got a packet of pictures of ball players in a gum wrapper. Later a girl gave him three more because she wasn't saving them. His friend traded him one for two he needed. Choose the correct arithmetic statement to show how many he will have. A number may be assigned to his original packet or an "X" may be used. To graduate the difficulty, teachers may begin with correct numbers in proper places and progressively change the order between the written numerals as they appear in the problem from the order of the printed numerals.

Algebra, geometry, and chemistry can be similarly introduced on a simple level. Guilford and Brown (1966) have stated that one purpose of the model is the generation of hypotheses which will test it. In the application of the SOI to school environments, this purpose can be accomplished by the teacher who generates tasks which fit model definitions (as she understands them) for the teaching of abilities within known subject matter. Perhaps one contribution of the model may be the creative experiences teachers gain in organizing methods of teaching and in exposing the child to experiences which stimulate him in heretofore untouched areas.

Exercises described above are particularly necessary in the fifth and sixth grades. During these years, drill and rote associated with facts-learning need to be amplified and diversified so that interest and motivation are retained. This is equally important for superior and gifted students who become bored with simple repetition but need conditioning of facts. These facts become easily accessible as rote responses and clear conceptually as prerequisites for algebra.

Evaluation: The Semantic Dimension

EVALUATION OF SEMANTIC UNITS (EMU) is the ability to make judgments about the suitability or adequacy of ideas and word meanings in terms of meeting certain given criteria.

Tests

Double Descriptions.   From four alternatives, select the one thing that fits two descriptive categories best. (32)
Sentensense. Judge whether a given sentence expresses internally consistent thoughts. (32)

The Minkus completion tests in the Binet, and similar items in the Henman-Nelson tap the EMU and EMR abilities, although both require a convergent production of the word omitted.

The Bennett Mechanical Comprehension Test, Form A, also tests this ability and has been considered successful for personnel selection where judgment is important.

Curriculum Suggestions

Children in primary grades enjoy a game in which the teacher makes a short sentence either misusing a word meaning or using a wrong word.

This "game" trains auditory attention and evaluative abilities at the same time, for the child must scan the limited meanings he has integrated or stored and make a judgment about the correctness of the word usage.

Investigation into the development of sense of humor is in its infancy (Wilson, 1968); this kind of game may not only train judgment but may, for those children who have not yet achieved finer shades of connotative humor, help them to do so. For those children who have, of course, the game can be hilarious.

Students in higher grades can be given a similar experience in the form of a visual presentation.

Secondary English teachers utilize, to a limited extent, the above technique when they present quotations from which their students must make interpretations.

EVALUATION OF SEMANTIC CLASSES (EMC) is the ability to judge applicability of class properties of semantic information.

Tests

Best Word Class.   Of four given class names, select the one to which the given object best belongs. (32)
Class Name Selection.   Select a class name that best fits a group of four given words. (32)

Curriculum Suggestions

The ability to classify is basic to the formation of concepts because it imposes an ordering and organizing of information into a manageable gestalt.

Classifying semantics evaluatively differs from other operations such as cognition in that the student must select the best fitting of class names given. It is as though there were a two-way "fitting" in the selective process. The classifying is not limited to single words or ideas.

Arithmetic problems offer opportunities for developing experiences wherein students learn to make judgments about the semantic or conceptual attributes of arithmetic problems. For example, addition and multiplication form one small class of procedures to problem solutions, whereas subtraction and division form a similar class of procedures. This type of approach to math has been more beneficial to students who can conceptualize theory behind computation better than they can perform the rote symbolic skills. This additional approach also exposes the theory to students who are good at following rules but who are not so capable in making judgments, breaking sets, or questioning rules in order to use them selectively at other times.

EVALUATION OF SEMANTIC RELATIONS (EMR) is the ability to make choices among semantic relationships based on the similarity and consistency of the meanings.

Tests

Verbal Analogies III. In an analogies format, the relations between the first two words are fairly obvious and the choice of alternative completions very difficult. (32)

Best Trend Name. Select the word that best describes the order of four given words describing a meaningful trend. (32)

Curriculum Suggestions

Students need to be given many experiences in analogical thinking before they are confronted with test problems. That is, analogical thinking should not occur as a new experience for them on the test if what is desired is a measure of their power or potential in this ability. Discussions at the simplest level can involve examples like: "When it is cold and snowing or raining, your mittens go on your hands like *what goes on your feet?*" Examples should fit the age levels of students.

EVALUATION OF SEMANTIC SYSTEMS (EMS) is the ability to judge the internal consistency of a complex of meaningful information.

Tests

Word Systems. Evaluate three matrices of words and indicate the one that shows the best trends and the one with the worst trends of words in both rows and columns. (32)

Unlikely Things. Select the two more unlikely or incongruous features from four given alternatives in sketches of common situations. (32)

Curriculum Suggestions

This ability is one which probably needs more stimulation than it usually receives in formal education. SOI profiles from Stanford-Binet responses of boys with behavior problems very often show deficits both in this (EMS) and the relations cell (EMR) (Meeker, 1966). Whether the lack of the ability to make accurate evaluations leads to behavior problems or whether the inability is a result of atypical or unacceptable behavior, is not yet established. Evaluative experiences in which there are alternatives from which to choose need to be provided for such children. Specifically the ability to evaluate needs to be taught. If the teacher is interested in developing correctness of social responses, a progression from figural-visual stimuli to auditory-vocal stimuli should be presented to these students.

Questions can be raised here as to where a systems product ends and implications and relations products begin; this is a difficulty if we desire to retain purity of factors. One speculation is offered toward an answer: For the child who already knows the correct alternative, the experience may be that of completing a system because he can foresee the implications; for the child who is not experienced and so must reason or guess, the experience becomes a relations one.

EVALUATION OF SEMANTIC TRANSFORMATION (EMT) is the ability to judge which objects or ideas could best be transformed or redefined in order to meet new requirements. These kinds of exercises are opportunities for originality with ideas and creative endeavors. Offer the child any practice in which he must first redefine the idea or object before he can perform the required task. This will acquaint him with one type of creativity.

Tests

Useful Changes.   Select the object that can perform the specified task most adequately, all alternative objects needing redefinition in order to perform the task at all. (32)

Curriculum Suggestions

Science will afford opportunities for exploration in this ability because so many units in the course of study are open to "what if" questions. In social studies, children can be required to imagine and describe how various services could have been performed differently had circumstances been different. Questions which force them to "break sets" in traditionally accepted institutions or folkways not only teach them alternative actions but also often lead them to understand why some changes are not helpful while others are. A questioning of the status quo most often brings about the acceptance of it.

EVALUATION OF SEMANTIC IMPLICATIONS (EMI) is the ability to judge adequacy of a meaningful deduction.

Tests

Complete Thoughts.   Judge whether a group of words expresses a complete thought or is a complete sentence. (32)
Sentence Selection.   Judge which conclusion is fully supported by a given sentence. (32)
Logical Reasoning.   Judge whether or not a conclusion follows logically from given premises. (32)
Items testing this ability are frequently found in all group intelligence tests at the elementary, high school, and college levels.

Curriculum Suggestions

Similar test items are frequently used by most teachers in English and social studies in the upper grades.

In the primary grades, teachers would most likely get better results if such questions were used in discussion groups and used more frequently. Many students report they "learned more" in speech than any other subject. It is in speech courses that time and opportunities to "think, question, and reason" are offered freely.

FIGURE 6-1
FACTORS IDENTIFIED IN CONVERGENT PRODUCTION

	Figural	Symbolic	seMantic	Behavioral
Units			NMU	
Classes	NFC	NSC	NMC	
Relations		NSR	NMR	
Systems		NSS	NMS	
Transformations	NFT	NST	NMT	
Implications		NSI	NMI	

6

Convergent-Production
Factors

Convergent Production: The Figural Dimension

CONVERGENT PRODUCTION OF A FIGURAL CLASSI-
FICATION (NFC) is defined as the ability to classify,
uniquely or conventionally, items of figural information. (In
the figural dimension [FIG. 6-1] only two clear factors have
emerged — NFC and NFT.)

Tests

One factor test has delineated this ability:
Figure-Concept Grouping. Given figures are classified so that
the attribute of each class formed is also an attribute of a
given target figure. (39)
    Similar exercises appear as tasks in Upton and Samson's
Creative Analysis (1963).

Curriculum Suggestions

    The importance of this factor for education most probably
lies more in the task of classifying rather than in the subject
matter to be classified. Numerals can be classified on the
basis of whether they are straight or curved; that is, the
numeral is detached from its acceptable meaning and becomes an object having other qualities. Geometric or other
code symbols can be presented for classification on the basis
of some similarity which differentiates one symbol from others
in a list. Experimental attempts can be made to classify
auditory presentations of visual symbols. The teaching of

sounds of letters and numerals can be approached from a singular classification point of view. This sort of classifying of sounds frequently occurs in oral discussions among reading groups in primary grades; more time should be devoted to classifications as tasks. Individual responses will indicate to the teacher whether or not the child really understands the concept. Those students who are confused need individualized help.

A psycholinguistic approach aimed at a rudimentary classification exercise can be tried with familiar poems. For example, students can pick out words which sound "light and airy" in the nonsense poem, "The Jabberwocky," from Lewis Carroll's *Alice in Wonderland:*

> 'Twas brillig, and the slithy toves
> Did gyre and gimble in the wabe:

Which words sound happy? Which words sound ominous?

Other kinds of figural information are available for classification besides sounds. Given various pictures, children can categorize them according to specified instructions. Pictures may be classified according to whether they are all trees, blue, round, or what the teacher feels the student needs to experience. The student who can then find the correct members for that class will have had an opportunity to learn and develop an ability to organize information.

CONVERGENT PRODUCTION OF FIGURAL TRANSFORMATIONS

(NFT) is the only other figural content which has been factored to date. It is defined as the ability to break down given figural units to form new ones. Locating faces or objects hidden in complex pictorial scenes describes this ability.

Tests

Penetration of Camouflage.   Locate faces hidden in complex pictorial scenes. (USAF) (34)
Hidden Figures.   Indicate which of five simple figures is concealed in each of the more complex Gottschaldt figures. (34)
Hidden Pictures.   Find human or animal pictures hidden in a complex scene. (LLT)

Curriculum Suggestions

The kinds of items which would give training in this ability are rarely encountered in group tests even at the primary level. The Frostig test does include a figure-ground discrimination subtest which may depend on this ability. Some commercial workbooks have a few pages of such exercises. *Children's Highlights* and *Humpty Dumpty* magazines include such a task in each issue. Children love to find the hidden pictures. Faces, animals, shapes, and words, letters, and numerals can be used. Relatively few opportunities occur where children can engage in this kind of "fun." The occasional reading-readiness and mental maturity tests which do present similar tasks are frequently new experiences for most children. Since it is a task predicated on a type of figure-ground discrimination ability and since it would subsume adequate visual perception, practice, or both, teachers finding students who lack this ability need to use such tasks as models for making seatwork. Since transformation also often taps creative ability, such tasks can be used to accomplish more than one goal.

Finding models, and reproducing them, will require researching magazines and writing for permission to reproduce the pages. High-school art students can be assigned a project to camouflage hidden letters and numerals. Figure 6-2 shows one example of such an assignment; figure 6-3 shows another using numerals.

FIGURE 6-2
CAMOUFLAGED LETTERS

FIGURE 6-3
CAMOUFLAGED NUMERALS

Convergent Production: The Symbolic Dimension

CONVERGENT PRODUCTION OF SYMBOLIC CLASSES (NSC).   The first cell to factor clearly in this dimension is that of classification. It is the ability to classify uniquely items of symbolic information.

Tests

Letter Grouping.   Group a given list of nonsense words into four classes, using each word only once. (39)
Restricted Symbolic Classifications.   Classify a given list of nonsense words so that each word is a member of two classes. (39)

Curriculum Suggestions

The fundamental difference here between Cognition of Symbolic Classes (CSC) and coNvergent production of Symbolic Classes (NSC) lies in the recognition of the classifications as opposed to reproduction of asked-for classes.

Letters may be grouped as nonsense words into prescribed classes. Or, a given list of nonsense words may be classified so that each word is a member of two or more classes. For example, place all the nonsense words that sound like a word into one class; place those that do not in another class.

CONVERGENT PRODUCTION OF SYMBOLIC RELATIONS (NSR) is the ability to complete a specified symbolic relationship.

Tests

Correlate Completion II. Discover the rule by which two pairs of words are related, then apply it to a third pair, completing it. (31)

Coding tests frequently require the examinee to decipher or "break" the code in order to translate the words.

Curriculum Suggestions

A question arises here as to why producing any number in a series of related sequences of numerals does not factor as a convergent task. One can only speculate that such a task reflects more as memory for a well-practiced operation than finding the relationship and applying it.

Action verbs can be paired in this manner as can inanimate objects. Nonsense syllables can also be used to train students to look for the relationships.

$$b \ k \ w - c \ l \ x \qquad \text{Which three letters}$$
$$\text{should follow?} \quad d \ m \ y$$

Developing codes and translating them are interesting tasks for individual homework or group projects.

CONVERGENT PRODUCTION OF A SYMBOLIC SYSTEM (NSS) is the ability to produce a fully determined order or sequence of symbols.

Tests

Operations Sequence. State the order in which a sequence of numerical operations should be performed in going from one number to another. (33)
Word Changes. State the order in which to place words in order from a given starting word to a given goal word, changing only one letter at a time. (33)

Curriculum Suggestions

The latter test offers a rich model for teaching reading from a psycho-linguistic viewpoint. It also may serve as a model for practice in writing and for conditioning spelling words which are unfamiliar to the student, for example:

Go from "applesauce" to "place," dropping one letter at a time.

(aplesauce, aplsauce, plsauce, plsace, place)

Arithmetic: To teach components of whole numbers. The worksheet shows several numerals such as 10, 4, 8, 16, ... The student is asked to show each number he would subtract in order to end up with a specified number, for example:

| 10 | _____ | _____ | _____ | _____ | 3 |
| 4 | _____ | _____ | _____ | _____ | 0 |

CONVERGENT PRODUCTION OF SYMBOLIC TRANSFORMATIONS (NST) is the ability to produce new symbolic items of information by revising given items.

Tests

These particular factor tests have received major use in theoretical explorations of creativity:

Camouflaged Words.   The reader is expected to find the name of a sport or game concealed in a sentence. (33)

Word Transformations.   Indicate new divisions between letters in the words of a phrase. (33)

These tests have served as models which have been used extensively in research on creative children both in schools (Getzels & Jackson, 1962; Gowan, 1963; Torrance, 1963) and in industry to select creative executives and engineers.

Curriculum Suggestions

Variations of the above tests may be used in various subject matters. The most valuable result of these tasks with children will probably come from the breaking of sets and the training in flexibility.

CONVERGENT PRODUCTION OF SYMBOLIC IMPLICATIONS (NSI) has been defined as the ability to produce a completely determined symbolic deduction from given symbolic information, where the implication has not been practiced as such.

Tests

Form Reasoning. Solve the simple equations that are given in terms of combinations of similar geometric figures. (33)
Sign Changes. Given the condition that certain numerical-operation symbols are interchanged, solve simple equations using the changes. (33)

The Semantic Test of Intelligence (STI-1952 Harvard University, Rulon, P. J.) interestingly enough uses *figural* stimuli which are learned as a new set of symbols and are then combined into short "sentences." The test acts as a coding, thus placing it in the Guilford symbolic dimension. The task is similar to that required for the solution in *Form Reasoning.*

Curriculum Suggestions

Sign Changes could serve as a model only under conditions in which negative practice was desired. It is not recommended at the elementary level.

Form Reasoning might perhaps be used as a model for more sophisticated levels (implications) in working with children who learn best through tying the figural stimulus to the semantic to make a symbolic language.

Neurologically handicapped students may benefit from using cut-out pictures as a notation system to develop a dictionary of meaningful symbols.

Convergent Production: The Semantic Dimension

CONVERGENT PRODUCTION OF SEMANTIC UNITS (NMU) is the ability to converge on an appropriate name (or summarizing word) for any given information.

Tests

Picture-Group Naming. Provide the class name for a group of five pictured objects. (39)
Word-Group Naming. Provide the class name for a group of five words. (39)
Naming Meaningful Trends (Seeing Trends I). Name the meaningful trend in a group of given words, where the order is not completely correct, but the trend is apparent. (39)

Curriculum Suggestions

Teachers will recognize this as a most common task and one which is most frequently used in any classroom when the one converging answer to any question is asked for either in oral participation or in written tests. Since this ability is almost synonymous with school achievement (grades), it might be taught less often in deference to tasks which train toward other abilities.

CONVERGENT PRODUCTION OF SEMANTIC CLASSES (NMC) is the ability to produce verbally meaningful classes under specific conditions and restrictions.

Tests

Word Grouping.   Given 12 common words, put them into four, and only four, classes, leaving no extra words.   (39)
Figure Concepts (uncommon).   Given a collection of pictured objects, combine them in classes, the score being the number of uncommon classes.   (4)
Largest Class.   Form the largest possible class of words from a given list so that the remaining words also form a class.

Curriculum Suggestions

This particular task, like other classification tasks, is seldom taught in school in the early grades. Yet we often assume that students can perform such tasks.

The ability to produce an additional "new learning" of classifying in conjunction with "new vocabulary," compounds the learning of a science or foreign language, and often makes the initial learning so much more difficult than it need be that students have a hard time recovering from the onslaught of "double learning." It is no wonder that they begin science in particular with such feelings of inadequacy that they come to dislike the subject.

It is apparent that tasks of classification are not simple and the convergence of the production of classes demands that the classification be made according to predetermined standards. It would be nearly impossible to separate the classifications involved in any science from its substantive body of knowledge except through emphasis and timing. Descriptions of sciences and languages could be so organized as to teach a classification scheme as introduction to the subject matter.

Many psychologists consider this kind of task to be the basis for concept formations in general.* Educators such as Russell** have stated that science, social studies, English, foreign languages, math, and specific language arts are all subjects in which preparation for assimilation depends on the ability to classify. If the assumption is made that the student has learned basic classifying techniques, and he has not, in fact, been taught how to classify or how to think in such terms, he may fail or achieve inadequately even though

---

*J. S. Bruner, J. J. Goodnow and G. A. Austin, *A Study of Thinking* (New York: John Wiley & Sons, Inc., 1956).
**D. H. Russell, *Children's Thinking* (Boston, Mass.: Ginn and Company, 1956).

his intellectual potential is good. Upton clearly expresses why this situation is the case.* He has developed exercises in *Creative Analysis* (1963) to alleviate the disability. Although this book was written for use by college freshmen and high-school seniors, it can properly be used with high-school seniors in English. It is suggested here that by teaching classification, beginning in the primary grades, we can eliminate, at the secondary level, the failures due to inexperience in this — a fundamental analytical ability.

CONVERGENT PRODUCTION OF SEMANTIC RELATIONS (NMR) is the ability to produce a word or idea that conforms to specific relationship requirements.

Tests

Inventive Opposites. Write two antonyms for a given word with the first letters of the responses being given. (LLT) (17)
Associations III. Produce a word that is similar in meaning to two other given words. (17)

Curriculum Suggestions

The former test item is rarely found in group tests; however, the latter, *Associations III*, is so commonly found and so frequently used by teachers and parents that there is no need for further description.
As we have progressed through the convergent-production matrix, it has become obvious why it has been dubbed the "School Block."

CONVERGENT PRODUCTION OF SEMANTIC SYSTEMS (NMS) is the ability to order information into a verbally meaningful sequence.

Tests

Picture Arrangement. Given four scrambled pictures of a comic strip, indicate the temporal order needed to make sense. (A) (34) Psychologists are familiar with, and recognize this test as a subtest in the WISC.
Sentence Order. Indicate the temporal order in which three events, if correctly placed, make sense. (34)
Temporal Ordering. List the appropriate order of steps to take to complete a project; for example, planting a new lawn. (10)

Curriculum Suggestions

There is a quality of "wholeness" in systems as the test descriptions indicate. The student, by reproducing the correct ordering from a beginning

---

*Albert Upton, *Design for Thinking* (Stanford University Press, 1959).

to an end, shows that he understands the ordering and totality of the given events.

Teachers can easily concentrate on a great many oral experiences centered around social studies units in the early grades where the students are introduced to the concept of ordering. Visual and vocal examples can be used. The difficulty of the task will be increased by requiring that each student contribute to the system under discussion. Vocal procedures act as introductory learning experiences, so that the student, when given pictured or written tasks, can be better prepared.

The California social studies unit in the course of study on *Home* includes an exercise of this type: The students walk around their school, draw maps of it and of their rooms and home, and discuss ways of going from one point to the other.

CONVERGENT PRODUCTION OF A SEMANTIC TRANSFORMATION (NMT) is defined as the ability to produce new uses for objects by taking them out of their given context and redefining them.

Tests

Gestalt Transformation.   Select one of five alternative objects, or parts of objects, to be used to serve a stated purpose.   (22)
Object Synthesis.   Name an object that may be made by combining two given objects.   (11)
Picture Gestalt.   Indicate which objects in a photograph will serve stated purposes.   (32)

Most reading-readiness tests incorporate items similar to those in the *Gestalt Transformation* test.

Curriculum Suggestions

Certainly originality or flexibility is called for in the successful performance of such tasks and so this particular kind of ability has been used to test creativity. Children create identical experiences for themselves both at home and outside of school because it is a "fun thing" to do. There are children's books which have horizontally separate sections, each of which turns independently, and by turning the different pages, the reader can make innumerable incongruous and funny stories.

The story-telling circle where each student adds his own contribution to a story provides a rudimentary transformational type of training.

CONVERGENT PRODUCTION OF SEMANTIC IMPLICATIONS (NMI) is the ability to deduce meaningful information implicit in the given information.

Tests

Sequential Association.   Indicate the best order for four words to produce a chain of associations. (22)

Attribute Listing II.   State the essential attributes of some object which will serve a certain purpose. (22)

Items such as these are rarely found in group tests. Tests of this sort aid personnel selection of engineers or executives where unique problem solutions are part of the job specifications.

Curriculum Suggestions

Variations of these tests can be explored by teachers within subject matters where students may be asked to list, either vocally or on paper, what the important requirements would be for any given problem situation. Again, implications thinking is a characteristic of creative people.

Exercises used to develop these tasks will prove difficult to grade as right or wrong, so perhaps fluency in responses, constructiveness, and logic in processes should be considered as more important than a letter grade.

FIGURE 7-1
FACTORS IDENTIFIED IN DIVERGENT PRODUCTION

	Figural	Symbolic	seMantic	Behavioral
Units	DFU	DSU	DMU	(I)*
Classes	DFC	DSC	DMC	(I)
Relations		DSR	DMR	(I)
Systems	DFS	DSS	DMS	(I)
Transformations	DFT	(I)	DMT	(I)
Implications	DFI	DSI	DMI	(I)

*Currently being investigated

86

7

Divergent-Production Factors

Divergent Production: The Figural Dimension

DIVERGENT PRODUCTION OF FIGURAL UNITS
(DFU) has been defined as the ability to produce many figures conforming to simple specifications.

Tests

Make a Figure. Given three lines; e.g., two short straight lines and a curved line, make different combinations in limited time. (35)

Make a Mark. Make simple figures of a specified kind; e.g., open figures composed of curved lines. (35)

Sketches. Add figural details to several replications of the same basic design to produce a variety of recognizable objects. (SPS) (35)

Dot Systems. Draw two copies of a given letter in different, relative positions within a matrix of equally spaced dots. (35)

Torrance (1962) developed the Minnesota Tests of Creativity for Children which were based on Guilford's test for this factor.

Several reading tests, such as the Metropolitan, have items similar to the *Dot Systems* test. The Frostig Test for perceptual motor skills also includes tests of this kind.

DFU tests rather precisely describe the characteristics of divergency as defined. That is, the solution to the problem may be unique but the processes involved in the solution demand deductive thinking in order to complete the task. Restrictions to the solution are few, and the search broad.

Curriculum Suggestions

This factor is also a "natural" for lessons in beginning art. The content on any sheet may be figures, shapes, letters, even words. Requiring that the end goal be recognizable places a constructiveness on the result. This offers useful exercises for students who need experiences in making better visual discriminations, since it forces them to take parts and combine them into wholes.

DIVERGENT PRODUCTION OF A FIGURAL CLASSIFICATION (DFC) is the ability to group figural information in different ways.

Tests

Varied Figural Classes.   Given a collection of three figural objects that can be conceived as representing different classes, which ones of five single figures can be classified with the three?   (35)
Alternate Letter Groups.   Find letters that belong to a class because of a commonality of shapes or figural elements.   (39)
Figural Similarities.   Use figural aspects of six complex figures to form classes of three figures each, based on some common feature.   (35)
Multiple Grouping of Figures.   Group and regroup a number of given figures into as many different classes as possible.   (39)

Curriculum Suggestions

The open-endedness of this task allows for individual differences in perception and may be used by the elementary teacher as a task to be assigned when certain classifications are pre-ordained as correct. Trading cards, pictures from magazines and papers are readily available and can be pasted on 3 x 5 cards.

The primary goal is to classify given stimuli; the divergency lies either in the ambiguity of the stimuli, the broadness of the possibilities of classification, or the flexibility of the scoring.

As Torrance (1962) found, it has been the scoring of the responses which has proved to be troublesome in the practical use of the tests; but scoring need not be the decisive factor for the teacher who is using the material as a task, not a test. If she decides to give her students experience in divergent classification, such tasks become seatwork rather than tests. In fact, for educationally, neurologically, and emotionally handicapped children, this kind of classification task may also be used to improve self-concept as well as to teach better discrimination. Here the student can feel safe, for his way is the correct way.

DIVERGENT PRODUCTION OF FIGURAL RELATIONS (DFR) has not been factored clearly and separately. As hypothesized by the model, the factor implies that the student would have the ability to generate relations

between figural items, relations which must be arrived at uniquely and organized constructively.

DIVERGENT PRODUCTION OF A FIGURAL SYSTEM (DFS) is the ability to produce composites of figural information in many ways.

Tests

There are three factor tests for this ability:
Making Objects. Given a few figures and lines, construct from them, with nothing added, specified meaningful objects. (SPS) (35)
Monograms. Given three letters, randomly, invent a variety of monogram designs. (35)
Designs. Given five figural elements such as a line, a curve, a dot, an angle, and a circle, combine them into designs that can appear on wall paper, linoleum, or fabrics. (35)

Curriculum Suggestions

Although this sort of task is usually reserved for art lessons, it can also be made a part of the curriculum at other times. Students can choose their own designs without referring to structured stimuli.

The test descriptions offer good models to be used for take-home gifts for Christmas, Mother's Day, Father's Day, ... Mentally retarded students and some physically handicapped have made stationery with such designs as letterheads. Irish potatoes and ivory soap are easily carved and make interesting prints.

DIVERGENT PRODUCTION OF A FIGURAL TRANSFORMATION (DFT) is the ability to process figural information in revised ways.

Tests

The tests for this cell include:
Match Problems II, III, IV, V. Given a set of adjacent squares or other figures of the same size, each line being composed of a match, take away a specified number of matches and leave a specified number of squares or triangles with no matches left over. Solve each item in as many as four ways. (SPS) (35)
Planning Air Maneuvers. Select the most direct path for skywriting letter combinations with an airplane. (USAF-M) (35)

The Horn Art Aptitude Inventory contains test items which measure aspects of DFT.

Curriculum Suggestions

It may be possible to give children experience in this ability in the first and second grades through the use of class members' own initials. Each child can put his initials on the board (or more than one can be chosen to do so) while the other members of the class make designs out of the posted initials. This can also be an introduction to geometric shapes and their labels. When students go to the board to make their designs, they receive eye-hand and spatial orientation training as well as perceptual training.

In a high-school senior honors English class the teacher became interested in teaching the SOI classification scheme. The students were assigned various cell descriptions and were required to produce a fitting example from school or home. The girl who received DFT reported she had a very hard time finding an example until she set the table. This is what she reported: Usually in her home the youngest of five, age 6, sat at the bar to eat for several reasons:

1. She often wanted to eat before the family did.
2. She was quite messy, and so it was more esthetic.
3. Their table was round and didn't accommodate five place settings.

At dinner time that night while she was getting the placemats it occurred to her that by making a figural transformation she could seat five. She changed the placemats

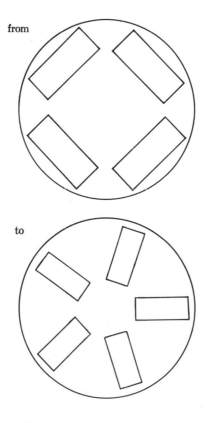

The whole family was amazed at the simplicity of the change—again, a breaking of set!

A fringe benefit for students may be the insight into the fact that there is more than one way to organize a group of figures, and all of them are acceptable. That is, fluency may be nurtured if the teacher feels that it has been depressed. This is certainly a partial answer to "can you teach creativity?"

DIVERGENT PRODUCTION OF FIGURAL IMPLICATIONS (DFI) is the ability to elaborate on figural information.

Tests

Factor tests for this ability are:
Decorations. Given articles of furniture or other objects in outline form, add decorative lines and markings. (SPS) (35)
Production of Figural Effects. Given a very simple line, build on the given information in order to produce a non-meaningful figure with some degree of complexity. (35)
Figure Production. This test is similar to the previous test, except that the student must produce a meaningful object. (35)
    This is another factor which has served as a test model for current research in creativity.
    Industrial firms use the Bennett Mechanical Comprehension Test which tests this ability.

Curriculum Suggestions

    Experiences which allow students to make implied additions to a given stimulus object are called "elaborations." It is probably easier to lead students to the understanding of inferred meanings by beginning with verbal elaborations.
    A demonstration might consists of the following: A box of objects collected by teacher and class members is at the front of the room. Each student can take a turn verbalizing ways to change an object or use it. The follow-up would consist of a sheet of drawings on which the student then makes his own changes.
    One exercise used successfully with gifted youngsters was the drawing of a square. The directions were: Draw what would be at the end of the square if the lines were extended into space out of sight. After the figural drawings were finished, two students verbalized their products and wrote the following poems.

CHILDHOOD

A Child's brief life is but a sugar cube
Of granules
Compressed into six quick walls of fantasy.
Imagination's tube
Is pliable, intriguing. Rises into falls.

Time lets no lingering. We must progress.
Our journey through this crystal maze is done
And sugar cube has melted in the sun
Of childish freedoms freely we possessed.

But please! One backwards, tear stained glance, then on.
We turn, we look, we reach; the child is gone.

THE CUBE

An inch is square and two dimensional.
Beyond the square evolves a cube from continued lines.
    (Or a rectangle.)
If one is without, then one is a spectator,
    a master in control.
Control of the length, the breadth, depth, and height.

Does the cube,
in its growth,
expand in time,
or does it narrow off into sightlessness?
If one could move at will over time
and pursue the cube,
what would be found beyond?
Constancy?
Changes in color or lines themselves?
And what if the atmosphere itself makes its own changes,
    unimagined yet?
And if the cube, pried open,
reveals . . .
Is there someone inside?
Close inspection answers who.
Close attention answers how.

Divergent Production: The Symbolic Dimension

DIVERGENT PRODUCTION OF SYMBOLIC UNITS (DSU) is the first product appearing in the symbolic dimension. It is the ability to produce many symbolic units which conform to simple specification *not involving meanings.*

Tests

Word Fluency.   Write words containing some specified letter. (SPS) (39)
Suffixes.   Write words ending with a specified suffix. (39)

Word Beginnings and Endings Tests.   Write words which begin with and end with specified letters.   (ETS)

Word Beginnings Test.   Write words beginning with a specified prefix. (ETS)

The Binet has only one item which tests this ability. One of the few timed tests, this item requires the examinee to vocalize a specific count of unrelated words in one minute.

Curriculum Suggestions

Fluency implies speed either in vocal retrieval from storage or speed in writing the words. Although fluency has been found to characterize certain creative adults, speed and timing too frequently have deleterious effects on young children. The same experiences should be given them without resorting to stringent timing. Speed should not be made the only criterion of success. With the pressure of speed removed, children are more likely to develop fluency and start gaining experience in divergency. Speeded tests were originally used for practical administrative purposes. Timing also allowed for a control in measurement; but when we are working with maturing organisms we need to keep in mind that handicaps of immaturity, anxiety, and "giving up" may well develop into negative personality or testing behavior.

DIVERGENT PRODUCTION OF SYMBOLIC CLASSIFICATIONS
(DSC) is the ability to group items of symbolic information in different ways.

Tests

Multiple Letter Similarities.   Indicate the different common properties that sets of letter combinations may have in common.   (39)

Multiple Grouping of Nonsense Words.   Form as many different classes as possible from a given list of nonsense words.

Curriculum Suggestions

Combinations such as letters, numbers, coding symbols may be used for similar classroom tasks. The teacher might want to use new vocabulary words, or sets of numbers being studied in the new math series, or telegraph or other codings, if the students are studying electricity or science. Again, the notion is that classification can be taught using regular course of study subject matter as components.

DIVERGENT PRODUCTION OF SYMBOLIC RELATIONS (DSR) is
the ability to relate letters or numbers in many different ways.

Tests

Letter Group Relations. Given a set of four letters that are related in several possible ways, select other sets of four letters that may have the same relations. (35)

Number Rules. Given a starting number, relate one or more numbers to it in various ways so as to achieve a given or prespecified result. (35)

Curriculum Suggestions

A small book, *Creative Teaching of Mathematics in the Elementary School,* by Alvin M. Westcott and James A. Smith, gives many examples of divergent methods. Filling in the *Magic Star,* familiar to most teachers, demands a divergent production of relations.

FIGURE 7-2
THE MAGIC STAR

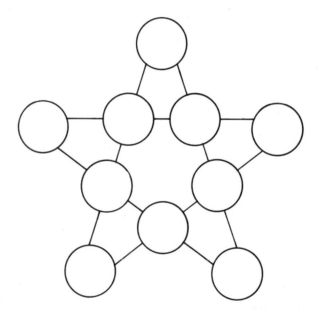

Each of the empty circles needs a number, 1-5, and all the numbers in each straight line must add up to 20. Can you find the right numbers?

DIVERGENT PRODUCTION OF A SYMBOLIC SYSTEM (DSS) is defined as the ability to organize sets of symbolic information into different systematic arrangements.

Tests

Make a Code test has factored separately for this cell. The task is the invention by the student of a variety of code systems in which he uses numbers and letters. He may use both or either separately as specified. (35)

Curriculum Suggestions

"There are 49 ways to make change for fifty cents. Can you figure them out?" Questions such as this may be applied to any number of specified amounts. Money and making change out of it or receiving change for it are as important to learn as language. Using the "change" concept, teachers can teach addition, subtraction, and other mathematical processes in a meaningful manner.

Kinesthetic experiences using fake coins and paper money make it questionable whether or not the task is in the symbolic dimension (it may be figural until the knowledge is integrated abstractly), but the divergent and system dimensions remain unchanged. There is a Merrigold booklet called *Many Pennies* which provides excellent experiences for children to learn kinesthetically and symbolically about numerical concepts and relations.

DIVERGENT PRODUCTION OF SYMBOLIC TRANSFORMATIONS (DST) has not yet been satisfactorily factored. However, it does seem that the ability, as hypothesized by the structure, is being partially tapped by the water jar problems—a symbolic activitiy in which the task involves getting the correct answer by transforming well-known operations.

The Binet does contain arithmetic items partially dependent on this ability. The examinee is asked to measure out so many cups, pints, or quarts of water using cans holding different amounts; he must be able to arrive at the correct answer by manipulating or transforming the measures conceptually. This kind of task also describes Piaget's "formal" thinking. The student must be able to break established arithmetic sets. How can he measure out nine cups of water using a seven-cup and an eight-cup can? The breaking of the sets requires flexibility at the transformational level.

DIVERGENT PRODUCTION OF SYMBOLIC IMPLICATIONS (DSI) is defined as the ability to produce varied implications from given symbolic information.

Tests

Limited Words. Given two common words, make a number of new word pairs from the letters included, using all the letters given. (35)
Symbol Elaboration. Given two simple equations involving letters, deduce a variety of other equations which follow from them. (35)

Curriculum Suggestions

This latter test offers a promising model for preparing children to learn algebra and logic. An effective series of exercises based on this ability could bring those children still in the concrete stage (Piaget) to the formal operations level by making meaningful the manipulation of relationships between abstract concepts using known components to establish associations.

Divergent Production: The Semantic Dimension

DIVERGENT PRODUCTION OF SEMANTIC UNITS (DMU) is defined as the ability to produce many elementary ideas appropriate to given requirements.

Tests

Ideational Fluency.   Write names of things fitting relatively broad classes; e.g., things that are white and edible. (SPS)   (37)
Topics Test.   Write ideas about a given topic. (ETS)
Theme Test.   Write as many words as possible about a given topic. (ETS)
Thing Categories Test.   List things that are round or that could be called round. (ETS)
Plot Titles (non-clever).   List appropriate titles for a given short story. (37)
Consequences (obvious). List consequences of a proposed unusual event; e.g., no babies born for one year. (SPS)   (37)
Utility Test (fluency).   List uses for a common brick and a common wooden pencil. (SPS)   (37)

Curriculum Suggestions

Variations of these tests can be used in many subjects. Fluency tasks allow the student to search his memory for unspecified numbers of materials and also give him practice in retrieving heretofore unassociated bits of information.

DIVERGENT PRODUCTION OF SEMANTIC CLASSES (DMC) is the ability to produce many categories of ideas appropriate in meaning to a given idea.

Tests

Utility Test.   List numbers of uses for a common brick. The scoring for flexibility shown in the ideas presented comes from the number of shifts of classes in the uses given. (SPS)   (39)
Alternate Uses.   List as many as six uses for an object, such as a newspaper, other than the common use which is stated. (SPS)   (39)
Multiple Grouping.   Arrange given words into different meaningful groups. (39)

Curriculum Suggestions

Variations of the *Utility Test* have been used in nearly every recent research on creativity in children. Industry, looking for creative executives, has also used this test in personnel selection. N. S. Maxwell, Sales Promotion Manager of Navan, a subsidiary of North American Aviation, Los Angeles, stated that selecting engineers who might have creative potential was only part of the problem. Another part concerned the training of these engineers to cope with designs and use transformations for by-products.

Divergency tests approach the measurement of creativity differently from traditional tests of artistic aptitudes. The latter tests (based mostly on evaluative judgments about which stimulus is better than its pair member) assume that talent is innate and needs to be identified. Divergent tests, because they measure different products across stimulus contents, give measures of abilities which may be components in a larger pattern of creativity. Both points of view have merit.

Guilford's basic assumption is that an ability can be developed. With this in mind, we can today expose children to experiences which may actually nurture and foster insights and component creative abilities.*

DIVERGENT PRODUCTION OF SEMANTIC RELATIONS (DMR) is defined as the ability to produce many relationships appropriate in meaning to a given idea.

Tests

Associational Fluency. Write synonyms for given words. (SPS) (37)
Simile Insertions. Supply a variety of appropriate words to fill blanks in a given simile. (37)
Controlled Associations. Write a number of synonyms for each given word. (11)

Most group achievement tests have similar items in the language sections. English achievement tests also stress this ability. It is frequently taught and tested for in language arts.

DIVERGENT PRODUCTION OF SEMANTIC SYSTEMS (DMS) is defined as the ability to organize words in various meaningful complex ideas.

Tests

Expressional Fluency. Given four initial letters with no word to be used more than once, construct a variety of four-word sentences. (SPS) (37)
Simile Interpretations. Complete in a number of ways a statement involving a simile, giving explanatory remarks. (37)

---

*The reader who is interested in measuring creativity for high-school students or industrial personnel is referred to the booklet, "Testing for Creativity," a reprint from *Machine Design,* May 27, June 10, June 24, 1965, Penton Publishing Co., Cleveland, Ohio, by Eugene Raudsepp, Princeton Creative Research, Inc., Princeton, New Jersey.

Word Arrangement. Write a number of sentences each containing four specified words. (17) A variation of this test also occurs in the Stanford-Binet.

Curriculum Suggestions

Any words the teacher wants to emphasize can be treated in either of the above ways: misspelled words, vocabulary (in English, science, or math), and similes.

DIVERGENT PRODUCTION OF SEMANTIC TRANSFORMATION (DMT)

is the ability to produce unusual, remote, or clever responses involving reinterpretations or new emphasis on some aspect of an object or situation.

Tests

Plot Titles (clever). Write titles for a short story; only clever titles being counted. (37)
Consequences (remote). Give remote (distant in time, space, or sequence of events) consequences for a specific event. (SPS) (37)
Symbol Production. Produce varied simple symbols to represent given activities and objects. (35)
Riddles (clever). Give clever solutions to riddles. (18) The Binet has several items which tap this ability.

Curriculum Suggestions

The most useful of these tests for school use is the *Consequences* test in which the student is asked to give remote (distant in time, space or sequence of events) consequences for a specific event.

Rainy-day sessions often find the teacher wishing for some game other than "Seven Up." The *Consequences* test offers a model for use then as well as at other more formal curricular times such as in social studies.

One student might give the event orally, a second, the remote in time response, a third, the remote in space, and a fourth, a remote in sequence event and on down the line until every student has had a chance to respond. You can expect some far-out consequences at the first few "loosening-up" times. Later, with practice, the students can write their own sequence, show more restraint and unusually clever answers.

DIVERGENT PRODUCTION OF SEMANTIC IMPLICATIONS (DMI)

is defined as the ability to produce many antecedents, concurrents or consequents of given information.

Tests

Planning Elaborations.   Add those detailed operations needed to make a briefly outlined plan succeed. (37)
Possible Jobs.   Suggest a number of different occupations or groups of people for which a given symbol or emblem might represent. (SPS) (37)

Occasionally mechanical aptitudes tests require answers to items similar to the *Possible Jobs* test; the Stanford-Binet has several questions which tap DMI.

Curriculum Suggestions

The requirement of producing many consequents, concurrents, or antecedents makes this an open-ended task which can be used for almost any teacher-determined subjects. There is a non-structuring in the possible answers, which gives the exercise a quality of flexibility in answers for solving the task; that is, the answer lies in the student's searching for possible precedents. Many of the "what if" questions posed by educators fit this description. It can be expected that responses from very young children might be limited and perhaps labored, but young children, too, can perform similar kinds of "free thinking," or at least be introduced to the fact that such activity has an acceptable place in the business of problem solving as well as in fantasy play. Let us take two examples of first graders.

In a privileged neighborhood: Robert came home from school. His big sister came home at the same time and read a note to him from their mother. It said to have a snack and play until she got home. She had gone with a neighbor to see a sick friend. Robert had a peanut butter sandwich and grape juice and then went to the garage to get his bike. When he got there he noticed that the car lights were on and getting dim and the car doors were locked. Why do you think they were on? How could he turn them off? (Say nothing about windows or extra car keys since these are alternative suggestions.) What might happen if he did not turn them off?

In an underprivileged school district: Robert was sitting on the curb watching the big kids play in the street. It was quiet for a moment, and then he heard water dripping. He followed the sound inside the apartment house and saw water trickling down the stairs from an apartment where the door was locked and no one was at home. No one was at home in his apartment either. What do you think happened in the apartment? What could Robert do? What would happen if he did nothing?

PART THREE

Interpretation and Uses for Curriculum Planning

8

Interpretation
of the SOI

An Information-Processing Model

The cube, representing the factor-analytic matrix of Guilford's Structure of Intellect (FIG. 1-1), like any other factor-analytic model is not a dynamic model of the learning process. The model is, of necessity, a static or structural one, resulting as it does from the statistical techniques used in multivariate analysis. It does, however, serve a taxonomic purpose and also indicates how information may interact and be interrelated. The way in which information is processed by a functioning person makes of this an acculturated model; that is, the model is composed of measures of abilities found repeatedly which categorize those paper-and-pencil test performances of persons in this culture.

With this qualification, the following speculations are offered to the reader. These explications interpret the model as a way of processing information; they have proved to be a facilitating means for the teaching of the model and for the assimilation of the information. It has always been difficult to show how the cube components are separate. Many readers lack skill in third-dimensional conceptualizations. In fact, third-dimensional conceptualization is one of the 120 SOI abilities, and because this has been such a difficulty, Guilford now laughingly refers to the cube as his "mental block."

Figure 1-1 shows the original cube derived from the statistical matrix. Figure 1-2 shows how the cube looks when the major operations are sliced apart, but is still in third dimension. Figure 1-3 takes each slice from the cube and lays it flat so that the five major operations are exposed in two dimension. When the cube is thus spread out, it is easier to see that the internal components of each of the operations are identical. In fact, it is this perspective of the SOI model which serves as a profile of individual SOI abilities. (See Chapter 11 containing profiles based on Binet and WISC responses.)

Referring to Fig. 1-3, let us look at it as a way of processing incoming information. That is, follow the arrows beginning with the one in the lower left-hand corner and note that the first operation to be tapped is that of cognition. This means that the person is receiving, or is aware of, stimuli impinging upon him from his environment. He is perceiving stimuli (contents) which may be figural, symbolic, or semantic in nature and which may be organized into any of the end products such as units, classes, relations, systems, transformations, or implications. It is at this point that we must leave the structural or static model and interpret the model as a way of processing and perhaps even as a way of organizing learning or knowledge. The arrows are drawn in Figure 1-3 to facilitate following the possibilities of this processing.

Once the organism has cognized or comprehended something in his environment, there are several courses of action available to him.

1. He may *not* store it in his memory; the processing stops there.

2. He may store the information in his memory but cannot keep it for long (short-term memory).

3. He may store the information in his memory permanently (long-term), but he may or may not use the material.

4. He may cognize information and (follow the arrows) evaluate it, or
   a) store it as cognized,
   b) forget it (not store),
   c) reproduce it as an answer (N—coNvergent production),
   d) add something from memory as an association and reproduce it as learned (N), or solve a problem uniquely (D—Divergent production).

5. He may cognize the information, reproduce it as learned (N—coNvergent production), and
   a) forget it (which too frequently occurs after tests), or (follow the arrows)
   b) store the information in his memory.

6. He may cognize information (follow the arrows), evaluate it, draw from memory for an associated fact and reproduce the material (follow the arrows) as it stands (convergent production), or reproduce it differently but constructively (divergent production) without seemingly making an evaluation. This may be one explanation for the rapid cognition and retrieval which characterize the "Aha" phenomenon.

There are, of course, other alternative ways to use these five major ways of processing information, and any combination, simple or complex, is available to the organism. The interesting and often speculated upon "Aha" phenomenon can also occur seemingly independent of routing or branching; that is, the individual suddenly produces an idea. Perhaps it did come with immediate cognition (C to D) or directly from memory. Perhaps it occurred during an evaluation (E to D) or after having reproduced a known product (N to D). The many possibilities are certainly interesting to contemplate.

From the psychologist's or teacher's point of view, the importance of considering the model as a way of processing information lies in assessing which areas need to be taught and applying that knowledge to the teaching process. If these intellectual performances are dependent on the kinds of information people need to know and handle in order to function intellectually in our society, then these should represent to a certain extent the kinds of abilities we ought to transmit to children.

The structure does not and should not postulate a fixed hierarchy of abilities, because to do so may negate the purpose of using a factor-analytic model for teaching. Neither is a hierarchy of developmental acquisition postulated. We do know that children as young as age two have many of the SOI abilities, because this information comes from many validation testings, and we can speculate about certain phases of development: Auditory stimuli (spoken words) are comprehended before their visual representations (written words), but this is true only up to a certain point when reading skills are mastered. We also know that children understand semantics auditorially before they understand symbols, even though a postulated mental age of 6.0 has traditionally served as an index in the schools to signal the teaching of semantics and symbols (reading and arithmetic) at the same time. In one sense, in the early stages of learning, semantics are more primitive than symbols even though the child may be able to cognize both before being able to internalize learning about them differentially. Nevertheless, there is a point at which, particularly in math, symbols are more simple than semantics (abstract), and again another point at which symbolic skills become much more complex than semantic skills. Which of these is more important to teach when?

All of these speculations suggest areas in need of investigation for an even more precise application of the structure. Impetus will be given particularly to studying these questions and deciding how the answers fit into the structure as a consequence of the validations currently going on about Piagetian postulations concerning the acquisition of knowledge. How do research ideas of other psychological investigators fit into Guilford's model?

A Proposed Schematic for Prescriptions in Educational Psychology

Robert Watson has outlined some of the functions psychological prescriptions should serve. He points out the need for articulating research from theory into application, and in so doing brings into syncopation thoughts of scientists, philosophers, and psychologists; his plea for a search of direction should produce nagging questions in the conscience of each reader.

Some of the most important psychological research of the past decade has largely been ignored, it is true, in its application to learning, both in terms of formal education contents and in the informal education milieu of the home. Guilford has contributed a static model of acculturated intelligence; Piaget has pioneered in the work of understanding developmental sequences in cognitive formations just as Gesell pioneered the charting of sequences of physical development. Many other psychologists have contributed and are contributing specific findings to support the general proposition that the full range of cognitive skills develop predictably in the process of intellectual maturation. Physiologists have long since provided salient differences between the adult and the child who superficially may look like a miniature adult. Developmental psychologists have shown us that the child intellect is not necessarily a miniature adult intellect, and although the child may have potentialities within the same total structure attributed to adult intellect, he may not have all the skills to a lesser degree. There are identifiable capabilities that, at given ages, he does not have at all.

As with many such "discoveries," when simply stated, they seem altogether too obvious; and yet there is ample evidence that these truisms have not been applied to the educational process. For the most part, the learning experiences that we provide for children confirm the fact that we are treating them as little adults. We tend to scale down adult expectancies rather than provide them with experiences appropriate to their developmental level or with those skills which are components in the sequence of expected abilities.

Educational and curriculum materials, like the miniature-adult attitudes about child development, have sprung from unarticulated folkways which have dictated education in general. Yet it has long been the acknowledged purpose of educational systems to change the behavior of children by instilling in them the kind of knowledge which is deemed important by the supporting culture. Each system going along in this way (even those which have employed learning analysts, the latest teaching machines, and programmed learning instruction) has found itself serving perhaps 60 or maybe 80 percent of its population adequately. But, with the extension of the age for compulsory education, so has each of these school systems been faced with the undeniable fact that a large percentage of children neither learns nor integrates knowledge successfully if it is taught in the traditional academic manner, even though this may suffice and be successful with the majority of students who learn. Certainly few students leave school loving to learn.

Each district, each state has then had to take a first step in the solution of this problem. They have had to place the seriously impaired children (neurologically handicapped, physiologically handicapped, mentally retarded, deaf, blind, and partial seeing, and now the emotionally and educationally handicapped) in special classes.

The second step does not make any changes. It has been customary to teach the traditionally accepted curriculum of each specific district to these special children. Special techniques may be employed differentially, but rarely is the curriculum itself changed. Perhaps the most unfortunate of all of these situations is the teaching of retardates. The goal still remains the same with changes occurring only in the methods of teaching the same subject matters. To this end, any visitor can see high-school retardates in almost any state trying to read the same primer or book they have read every year for nine years.

Even for the normal child the situation remains unchanged. Look at the most elementary experiences of an informal educational nature that we now provide for children. Most children's toys or experiences are commercially determined by toy manufacturers soliciting through communication media. For example, there are no formal experiences outside the laboratory that provide the child with color experiences in their simplest form. (Learning colors is a primitive conceptual classification ability.) The most frequent way of teaching color discrimination is through pictures. Occasionally large simple pictures with broad areas of solid color can be found, but pages of one solid color can never be found in a book. There is no question as to which is the better vehicle for color discrimination, not only for the normal infant, but also for the child with visual, intellectual, or other neurological problems. The picture book persists because it is a scaled-down adult experience and the solid color page is not—it is too simple. All due credit is given to the fine artists and humorists who design early level books, but this is a telling example of the discrepancy between looking at the child as a developing intellect and of looking at him as a miniaturized adult. Generalize this statement and situation to the findings of developmental and experimental psychology and it means that we should provide learning experiences geared to the child's cognitive development regardless of age.

Toward this goal, the simplest experiences are often the most needed. For many children, the transition to more complex skills is easily made so that the importance of the simpler experiences is obscured or at least minimized. For special children who do not make this transition rapidly (and estimates of 40% are said to be low by many learning disabilities experts), there are relatively few educational tools designed specifically for him, and his disabilities are only tentatively diagnosed and hardly ever placed in the total spectrum of organized thought development. Nevertheless, no matter whether the development of any child is rapid and facile or slow and tortured, we still have expectancies for the child that clearly presuppose rudimentary skills he may not have developed, based on primitive experiences which have never been clearly presented.

It is not a simple matter to give a child a simple experience. A simple experience, clearly presented, is as pure an experience as one can desire. A chain of experiences within an organized model of human abilities can, when given, lead to the development of complicated behaviors. This latter statement is well documented for Skinner's conditioning paradigm through the work of Bijou, Blake, Lovass, Moss, Simmons, and others, who have conditioned intelligible responses with autistic and severely retarded children. These investigators have worked from a single, almost cell-like quality of human response to a complicated cell-assembly-like response. They have found that even autistic children have very different acquisition curves of learning.

At the other end of the continuum of human behavior is Guilford's structure-of-intellect model, which has demonstrated consistently the measurable separation of factors (or acculturated abilities) found repeatedly in paper-and-pencil tests. Other investigators and theorists have hypothesized how these abilities come into being. No one knows definitely how, or when, these abilities come into being; no one knows whether or not children are "born" with such abilities, although Fantz and other investigators who are studying infant stimulation are coming close to some of the answers. We do know that environmental stimulation can develop some of the abilities that did not exist before.

The schematic shown (FIG. 8-1) represents an attempt to show the organizations of human abilities; it is a first attempt to relate findings in psychology by major theorists to the spectrum of acculturated abilities as found by Guilford. The schematic is speculative and not intended to be more than an attempt at the large picture within which psychologists must prescribe. It is organized to show the formation of percepts as they relate to end-goal achievements. A schematic such as this is helpful for three reasons: (1) it allows for development of training and teaching materials to be based on well researched premises, (2) it allows for identification of deficit areas which are in need of remediation as they relate to other abilities, and (3) it organizes the separate modal functions into levels.

Figure 8-2 shows where Bloom's *Taxonomy of Educational Objectives* categories fit into the SOI. The taxonomy uses broad descriptive categories, and in the preciseness of the structure definitions, these broad categories overlap as shown.

Comparisons of test coverage by the Binet, WISC and ITPA are designated within each operation and are coded to show the range of abilities being tested.

The SOI and Individual
Tests of Intelligence

Experts in remedial reading have always used reading tests as diagnostic indications for specific training. Should they find, for example, that a lack of word attack skills is the cause of the reading problem, then the student is taught those skills which will remove his deficit. On the other hand, psychologists who give tests specifically for information which is to be used as part of a case study can benefit from approaches used by reading diagnos-

FIGURE 8-1

A SCHEMATIC REPRESENTATION OF ACCULTURATED ABILITIES* WITH HYPOTHESIZED PERCEPTUAL AND CONCEPTUAL PREREQUISITES FOR DEVELOPMENT

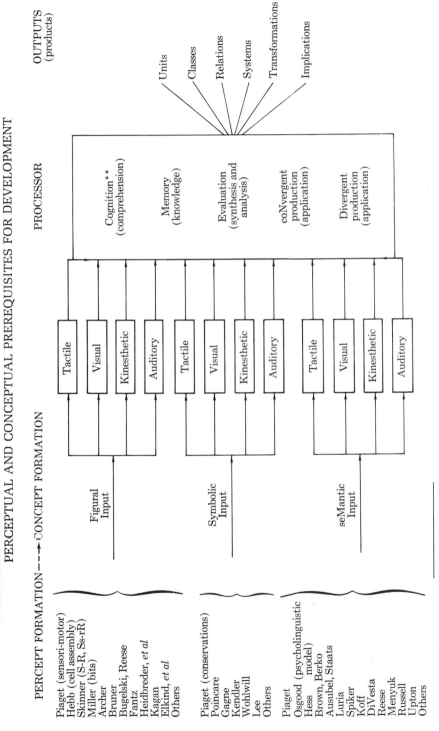

*Guilford's Structure of Intellect (SOI), 1956.
**Inclusive of taxonomy synonyms. Bloom, ed., *Taxonomy of Educational Objectives: Cognitive Domain* (New York: David McKay Co, Inc., 1956).

109

FIGURE 8-2
GUILFORD'S STRUCTURE OF INTELLECT
With A Flow Diagram of The Processes

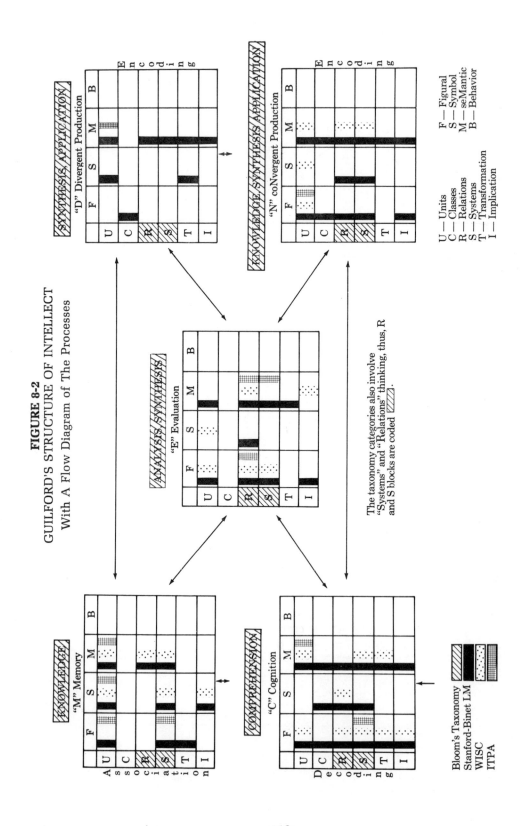

ticians. In intelligence testing, there are times when school psychologists can and should use intelligence-test results diagnostically—the child should be so taught as to eradicate a specific disability or deficit found in his intellectual responses.

Therefore, when Guilford (1956) suggested that there might be as many as 120 identifiable factors making up intellectual performance, this indicated to the writer that intelligence testing for educational purposes might well be reconstructed.*

It was anticipated then that some Binet and WISC users who previously had worked, at least quantitatively, with a single, molar measure of "intelligence," would have varied reactions to this exploding of a Binet or WISC IQ score.

The Binet and the verbal part of the Wechsler similarly tap heavily, though inferentially, the capabilities of individuals to acquire those symbols considered to be important for communication and cultural performances.

The competent psychologist has long sought to structure reactions and performances observed while a youngster is being tested. His attempts along this line have resulted in observations regarding the child's vocabulary level, his verbal conceptualization, his verbal and quantitative reasoning ability, and his memory.

Perhaps the most sophisticated attempt to make individual patterns out of observations during testing was that of Jastak (1939). He used a model of concentric circles with radii stemming from each center. The radii were labeled with subtest names. He showed three models of identical IQ scores; he connected the score points on each radius to show the individual differences in strengths and weaknesses. Intuitively and empirically Jastak searched for clarity and distinction in intellectual patterns.*

The school psychologist today should seriously ask himself these questions: "What kind of intellectual behavior does the Binet sample? How are these behaviors relevant to success and failure in school subjects? Are the abilities reflected in Guilford's SOI being sampled by the Binet?"

If the Binet were found to sample in any significant way any of the 120 ways of behaving, then the Binet would be more valuable than even its proponents had previously believed; it could have value not only in a molar manner—in reflecting a mass, undifferentiated learning potentiality—but also in such a way as to permit certain important differentiations in intellectual behaving. At the same time, these SOI samplings, if validated, would benefit from the reliability and validity of the Binet LM and WISC, and clinically competent school psychologists consistently would get more information out of the Binet than global scores of MA and IQ. This would be possible if Binet responses were known to be validly anchored in an integrated and precise conception of the intellect. The procedure described here

---

*M. Meeker, Paper presented at APA, Philadelphia, 1963.
*Citation with examples is shown in *Fundamental Concepts in Clinical Psychology,* Shaffer & Lazarus (1952), pp. 132-33.

is the product of work to this end. In fact, as will be seen, the procedures described here can be employed with respect to any device purporting to measure school learning aptitude, whether individual or group.

Validation

The author began implementation of this kind of research with the logical assignment of Binet items to the SOI. (SOI definitions were used as guides.) The first experimental draft was published by Los Angeles County, 1963. It was apparent after this attempt that further validation would not depend alone on the accuracy with which each item was characterized in terms of Guilford factors. That is, persons who understood the kinds of intellective processes sampled by each Binet item had to identify judgmentally those factors which properly describe it, and this was a problem of intra-or inter-judge reliability.

Inter-judge reliability presented a twofold problem: Those people who have a working knowledge of the Binet do not necessarily know the structure; conversely, those who know the structure best do not necessarily have a working knowledge of the Binet or what the items require the examinee to do. A factor identification procedure was necessary in order to permit the latter group to make a conceptual contribution and the former group to make a judgmental contribution. Obviously, another step had to be taken: Either performance on each item needed to be correlated with performance on the tests initially used in the identification of the factors involved, or a factor analysis of performance on Binet items needed to be made to see if those factors emerged which had judgmentally been determined to be involved. Toward the first alternative, a validity study was conducted by Philip Merrifield to see whether or not children who scored high on the factors thus identified also scored proportionately high on those same factors in Guilford's tests. His preliminary investigation was reported in 1963 at the American Psychological Association Convention in Philadelphia. Based on data taken from the Binets (L and M forms) of children in the pilot study of gifted children in California, Merrifield's findings indicated essential substantiation; a test-retest study included children matched in regard to age, sex, grade, and score.*

A Mapping Procedure for Assigning Test Items to the SOI and Illustrative Applications

We might first take a look at what we hope to gain by developing a mapping procedure. First, a computer program could be written for the

---

*Some of the data used for this study were taken from Elnora Schmadel's unpublished dissertation, "The Relation of Creative Thinking Abilities to School Achievement" (Los Angeles: University of Southern California, 1960).

procedure. Second, considering the Stanford-Binet, there is an advantage in mapping an instrument which has a history of such high validity and reliability. The value of capitalizing on these attributes of the Binet are real for educators who have made, are making, and will have to make predictions about educational performance. This is particularly so as knowledge increases and populations increase; they will be required to predict and also to decide how best to teach students. Third, research attempting to contribute definitive information about intelligence, and specifically about individual intellectual aptitude, needs to be rooted in the kind of stability the Binet offers. Conversely, the Binet needs to be rooted in a stable model or theory of intelligence. The main shortcoming of using the Binet has always been its yield of a unitary score. The fourth advantage of looking at the construct of intelligence in this way is the practicality of using a concrete tool which can be related more precisely to curriculum tasks, thus improving upon the "intellectual snapshots" which the teacher has been given of her pupils.

When the State of California, in 1961, legislated funds to be used by individual school districts for the special education of its gifted children (score of 130 or more as achieved on an individual test such as the Stanford-Binet or WISC), there was the problem of identifying these children and also of specifying the sorts of academic opportunities which would best benefit each child's individual abilities. This latter could hardly be derived from a unitary score of an identifying instrument; and yet, ironically, the individual testing situation represented one of the most intensive assessments of abilities in the child's history. Obviously a great deal was being lost for the child, the teacher, and the program.

The following mapping procedure was first presented in the Journal of School Psychology (1965).* It is offered as a practical tool for analyzing separate intellectual abilities as they would appear in Guilford's model. Whereas the Guilford tests, designed specifically to measure factors in the structure, would be "cleaner" tests of the specific factors for adult students (the tests have not yet been scaled down for younger students).** The time involved in such testing would usually preclude their use. By contrast, the mapping procedure offers a means of gaining some insight into these same factors.

In order to place each successive Binet item (1960 Stanford-Binet L-M is used as a consistent frame of reference) into its "correct bin" in the structure, it was necessary to arrive at some standardized way to select the appropriate cell out of the 120 possibilities. The logical analysis consists of a tree of questions which, by the direction of "yes" and "no" answers, automatically leads to the first, second, and third letters of the trigraph (for that cell or factor) which best fits the test item. (See figures 8-3, 8-4, and 8-5.)

---

*In *Journal of School Psychology,* 3, No. 3 (1965), 26-36.
**Most of the factors have been found to exist as abilities in children aged two and up. For a complete review of factors found in young children the reader is referred to Stott and Ball's book, *Evaluation of Infant and Preschool Mental Tests* (Detroit: Merrill-Palmer Institute, 1963). An unpublished work ongoing with Inta Ridler at the University of Toronto Institute of Child Study, 45 Walmer Road, Toronto, Canada.

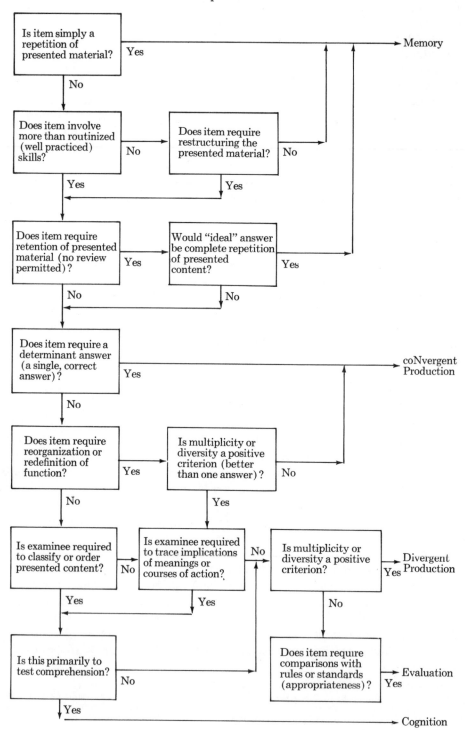

FIGURE 8-3
DECISION FLOW CHART
Operations

Is item simply a repetition of presented material? — Yes → Memory

No ↓

Does item involve more than routinized (well practiced) skills? — No → Does item require restructuring the presented material? — No

Yes ↓ (left box) Yes ↓ (right box)

Does item require retention of presented material (no review permitted)? — Yes → Would "ideal" answer be complete repetition of presented content? — Yes

No ↓ No ↓

Does item require a determinant answer (a single, correct answer)? — Yes → coNvergent Production

No ↓

Does item require reorganization or redefinition of function? — Yes → Is multiplicity or diversity a positive criterion (better than one answer)? — No

No ↓ Yes ↓

Is examinee required to classify or order presented content? — No → Is examinee required to trace implications of meanings or courses of action? — No → Is multiplicity or diversity a positive criterion? — Yes → Divergent Production

Yes ↓ Yes ↓ No ↓

Is this primarily to test comprehension? — No → Does item require comparisons with rules or standards (appropriateness)? — Yes → Evaluation

Yes ↓

→ Cognition

114

FIGURE 8-4
DECISION FLOW CHART
Contents

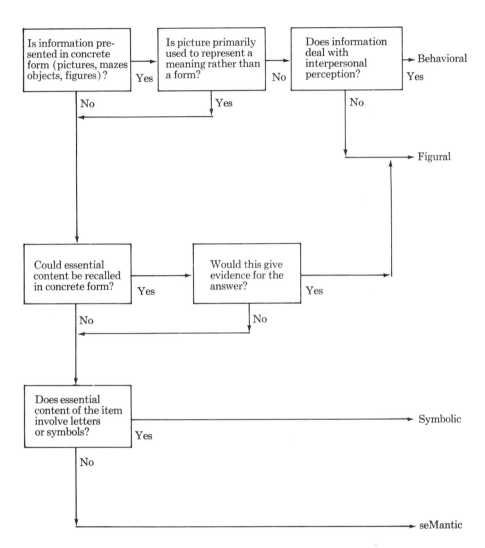

The relative "impurity" of the Binet items presented another series of problems. Certain items involve only one of Guilford's 120 factors. Others involve primarily one factor and secondarily one or more other factors. Still others, especially at the upper levels, seem to involve equally two or more factors. It looked as though many items required not one run through the screening, but several, in order to ascertain which type or types of intellectual abilities were being tested. Consequently, multiple cells were needed for many test items if they were to be judged exactly. On the other hand, certain limitations on multiple classification seemed appropriate. Although

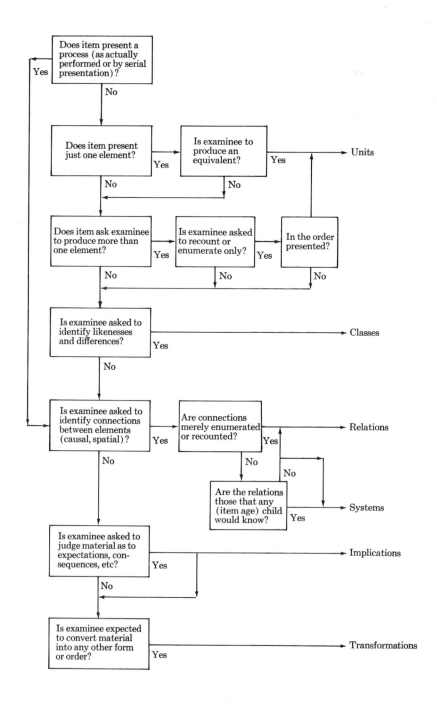

FIGURE 8-5
DECISION FLOW CHART
Products

Does item present a process (as actually performed or by serial presentation)?

Yes

No

Does item present just one element?

Yes

Is examinee to produce an equivalent?

Yes → Units

No

No

Does item ask examinee to produce more than one element?

Yes

Is examinee asked to recount or enumerate only?

Yes

In the order presented?

No

No

No

Is examinee asked to identify likenesses and differences?

Yes → Classes

No

Is examinee asked to identify connections between elements (causal, spatial)?

Yes

Are connections merely enumerated or recounted?

Yes → Relations

No

No

Are the relations those that any (item age) child would know?

Yes → Systems

No

Is examinee asked to judge material as to expectations, consequences, etc?

Yes → Implications

No

Is examinee expected to convert material into any other form or order?

Yes → Transformations

every item involves visual or auditory cognition, items were not classified as such unless this factor represented the *major* facet of the task for a given item. And, similarly, since auditory memory is also involved in almost every item, it is classified as a memory item only if the required response is primarily an assessment of recall ability. In all, the classification reflects the primary, as opposed to the necessary but peripheral abilities, required for correct response.

Statisticians are aware of the large variation in reliability between cells estimated from the Binet. Most of the variation results from differences in numbers of items representing different cells.

For a detailed explication let us take Year XI on the Binet, an exemplary year in terms of classification, and follow each item as we proceed through the decisions that have to be made. The factor designations and definitions which have been made by the author are presented to serve as a reference in this book in place of the actual Stanford-Binet. These are presented for all six items at Year XI, but the procedure for deciding which factors are involved is illustrated for only three items.

TABLE 8-1

YEAR XI	TASK	CELL AND DEFINITION
Item 1:	Graphic reproduction of a geometric figure	MFU Defined as recall of materials learned by visual and auditory presentation
Item 2:	Explaining why certain statements are foolish or ambiguous	EMS Recall of complex interrelated ideas in order to judge which ideational elements are inconsistent or incongruent EMR Sensitivity to choices among semantic relationships
Item 3:	Defining abstract words	CMU Comprehension of meanings of words
Item 4:	Repeating a sentence presented orally	MMS Immediate recall memory for an exact temporal order of words
Item 5:	Not only solving but also understanding the solution to a specific problem situation	CMI Anticipates needs or consequences of a given situation

YEAR XI	TASK	CELL AND DEFINITION
Item 6:	Finding the underlying relationship between verbal items as well as reclassifying them	CMT Sees several meanings to a word NMC Forms correct groups from a larger group of a class which is more meaningful

We shall now go back to Item 1 in order to see how this item would be assigned to its cell allocation in the Decision Flow Chart (figures 8-3, 8-4, 8-5). The examinee is asked to reproduce a figure. The first question to be asked concerns *Operations:* Is the item simply a repetition of presented material?* Answer: *Yes*, follow arrow to Memory. This gives the first letter in the trigraph (M). One might contend here that motor skill is the skill being tested on this item, and that it is normal for a child of eleven to be able to reproduce the given figures. However, the assumption the writer makes here, analyzing further, is that the item is not asking the subject to draw the figure with it before him, but rather is asking him to remember the complex shape, thus placing the item in an intellectual area (memory) which takes precedence over the involvement of motor dexterity.

To arrive at the second letter in the trigraph, it is necessary to look at the *Contents* portion of the chart.

1.   Is the information presented in concrete form? The answer is *Yes*. Following the arrow for *Yes*, we come to the question:

2.   Is the picture used primarily to represent a meaning rather than an object? The answer is *No*, so we follow the arrow to the next question:

3.   Does the information deal with interpersonal relationships? The answer is *No*, and the resultant letter is (F).

To arrive at the third letter in the trigraph for Item 1, turn to the *Products* portion of the chart.

1.   Does item present a process? *No*. Then, follow arrow.

2.   Does item present just one content element? Answer is *Yes*.

3.   Is examinee to produce an equivalent? Answer is *Yes*; then the third letter is (U) for Units.

Thus, MFU is arrived at, describing the behavior sampled by this item.

Item 2 at age eleven specifies that the subject explain why a given statement of a situation is absurd. As before, we start by finding the answers to the questions under *Operations* in the chart:

1.   Is the item a simple repetition? *No*. Does the item involve more than routinized skills? *Yes*.

---

*Readers who are familiar with the structural model will probably find it more efficient to evaluate *contents* first, *products* second, and *operations* last. The sequence followed here goes from "What does S do?" to "What does he do it with?" to "What is the nature of the end result?"

2. *Yes*, then, takes you to the question: Does item require retention of presented information? Answer is *Yes*, but that is not the "ideal" answer. *No* then asks:

3. Does item require reorganization or redefinition of function? *Yes*. Then, is multiplicity of response with a different answer necessary? The answer is *Yes*.

4. *Yes* takes you to: Is examinee required to classify? *No*.

5. Is examinee required to trace implications of meanings? *Yes*, and this leads to the question:

6. Is this primarily to test comprehension? *No*. Then is multiplicity a positive criterion? *No*.

7. This leads to Evaluation: Does item involve comparisons with appropriateness of practices? *Yes*. This produces (E).

Item 2 has (E) for the first letter. To ascertain the second letter, we look at the *Contents* portion of the chart.

1. Is information presented in concrete form? *No*.

2. Following arrow, could essential content be recalled in concrete form? *No*.

3. Does the essential content of the item involve letters? *No*.

4. Then the content is semantic, yielding (M).

To arrive at the third letter in the trigraph for Item 2, look at the *Products* section of the chart:

1. Does item present a process? *Yes*. Follow arrow.

2. Is examinee required to identify connection between elements: causal, spatial, functional? Answer is *Yes*.

3. More than one such element? Here we come to a critical junction. We are testing two levels. On the one hand, only one element is related to another. This implies a relationship, but the task does not ask that the relationship or connections be enumerated, for they are basic relations that an eleven-year-old would be expected to know; therefore, a system of thinking is involved, giving (S). Since more than understanding the system is necessary, and the item specifies that the child see the incongruencies, we go back to the branching point and answer *Yes*. Examinee is asked to judge presented material according to relationships (R).

We thus have both an EMS and an EMR as characterizing Item 2 at the XI year level.

Item 6 requires the subject to discover similarities among words. Following this procedure which has been illustrated, we turn first to *Operations*:

1. Is item a simple repetition? *No*.

2. Does item involve more than routinized skills? *Yes*.

3. Does item require retention? *Yes*, but not as the solution.

4. Does item require a determinant answer? *Yes*. This leads us to coNvergent Production. However, a comprehension of meanings is also necessary and *primary* to solving the problem. We therefore have cognitive ability involved (C).

So we have at least two kinds of major processes: coNvergent Production and Cognition. To arrive at the second letters, we find both tasks involve seMantics; thus we have (NM) and (CM).

The *Products* section will help in identifying the third letter. The first question requires that vocabulary be involved as one content element necessary to the solution, and, although examinee is not asked merely to recount in the order presented, he must produce an equivalent. Therefore, we obtain the third letter for the trigraph to denote the factor involved (U). Thus, we have CMU which is necessary but not sufficient, and seems subsumed in another cognitive ability. We must determine which other process is also involved, already having, as a start, the (CM) part of our trigraph.

1.   Is examinee required to identify connection between elements? *No,* not specifically. Is he then asked to judge presented material according to expectations? Again, not specifically as presented. Following the arrow at *No:*

2.   Examinee is asked to convert presented material into another form or order. *Yes,* so a transformation ability is being asked for, and we have a second type of cognition, CMT.

We now go through the process similarly in order to see what kind of convergent production is involved. The child is required by this item to reorganize meanings. Abbreviating the analysis a bit, we find the following:

1.   Midway down in the *Operations* portion of our chart, we find described the behavior this item intended to elicit: "require a determinant answer, a specified solution," which yields (N).

2.   At the lower portion of the *Contents* section, one item is appropriately described, in that "the essential content of the item involves letters," yielding the second trigraph letter (M).

3.   Under *Products,* halfway down, we recognize that what the child is expected to do in this item is "to identify likenesses and differences (common properties between or among elements)," which yields (C).

Thus it appears that this eleven-year-level item involves the joint operation of three of Guilford's factors, CMU, CMT, and NMC.

It becomes apparent that very concise judgments are required in the appraisal of the item, and that keeping the parts of the item separated while following a portion of a "thread" demands a high degree of compartmentalizing.

A major concern was the quantification of vocabulary. Should, for instance, a performance on Vocabulary (CMU) be regarded in terms of having been identified as high as, say, the eleven-year level, or in terms of having been passed as Vocabulary at each level? It may be that the purpose of any given study of the child will determine which is more meaningful, but for the present the latter method has been selected, giving the same balanced weight to vocabulary as is the procedure in the Binet at each age level.

Since educators are obligated today to gain more knowledge about the individual student if that student's performance in school is to yield maximum payoff in helping him meet the demands of the future, it is possible that, if the Binet can be used for the purpose of ascertaining parameters of abilities, we might hope to predict what these parameters are for an individual, provided we can relegate items to, and contain the test within, a model or theory of intelligence such as that postulated by the Structure of Intellect. If this is possible, then, this model of human intelligence should provide us with a contemporary pattern of the individual's abilities.

This assignation of Binet behavior samplings to the SOI was one step. The next step was the developing of templates which could be placed over the Binet to assign individual successes and failures to be plotted into an SOI profile. This should be a practical procedure and should have the added advantage of capitalizing on the validity and reliability of the Binet.

Logic for this approach can be summarized as follows: Teaching goals demand that the learner have abilities for certain tasks, and these abilities may cut across all tasks in much the same manner as the "pervasive 'g' factor" in general intelligence runs through the Binet (Cronbach, 1960). Separate abilities are defined by the Structure of Intellect. An appraisal of these separate abilities as defined by the structure and contained within the Stanford-Binet might show consistent patterns for each child. The consistency could exist in the failing or passing of semantic, symbolic, or figural content and/or on any product level and/or within any major process. A graphic representation of any child's pattern of abilities which directly relates to curriculum tasks would make educational planning for him realistic, practical, and rewarding.

This mapping procedure has been presented in order to show how intelligence test items have been characterized in terms of factors in Guilford's "Structure of Intellect."

9

Templates

Stanford-Binet LM

The templates for the Stanford-Binet (LM), WISC, and WPPSI are presented in this chapter.* They have been developed as a result of validations based on the mapping procedure.

The templates fit each test booklet page. Cell assignations are lined up with the numbered items as they appear in the test through the windows in the templates. (Cut out windows in the templates where the words "cut out" appear.) A flow diagram of the SOI is needed for each test administered in order to derive an individual profile. Accumulated expectancies for operations can be charted to derive a gross factor count.

Instructions: How to analyze the Stanford-Binet for given SOI factors

1. Place template over page to correspond with the basal age. Using "minus" (—) for incorrect, and "plus" (+) for correct, tally items from the window in the template to same cell or cells in flow diagram.

3. Continue scoring + or — through ceiling. Test form can be returned to files and the profile used independently. With practice, this clerical task can be performed in 3 to 5 minutes.

---

*The templates are available from M. Tolson, 6233 West 83rd Place, Los Angeles, California 90045.

4. Use another color for plotting ceiling items. Different colors can be used for responses at each year if finer distinctions are desired.

5. Count the plus signs in each major operation. Add them to the number of responses shown at the year *below the basal* in Table 9-1.

Interpretation

1. Is any one of the five operations (cognition, memory, evaluation, convergent production, or divergent production) stronger or weaker than others? If so, how does this relate to his achievement in school?

2. Is he passing or failing in any horizontal dimension in one or more of the operations (units through implications)? Where are his strengths and weaknesses? Should the teacher orient curriculum toward his weakness, or should the approach be through his strength? Might this pattern account for his problem in academic achievement? For gifted, which dimensions are strongest? Where are his weaknesses, if any?

3. Is he passing or failing in any vertical direction? Is he strong in symbols but weak in semantics or vice versa? For example, if he is strong in symbols but weak in arithmetic, why? If he is poor in the semantic area, is it at the concrete (units) level only or at the implications level only? Is it a general weakness? English and language arts can be taught to him depending on whether it is vocabulary weakness or abstract meanings weakness.

4. Individual deficits can be programmed for by teaching material designed according to the cell definitions.

FIGURE 9-1
TALLY SHEET FOR STANFORD-BINET (LM) TEMPLATES

Child's Name _____

I.Q. _____

STRUCTURE OF INTELLECT PROFILE
With a Flow Diagram of the Processes *

"M" Memory

	F	S	M	B
U	MFU	MSU	MMU	
C				
R			MMR	
S	MFS	MSS	MMS	
T	MFT			
I		MSI		

"C" Cognition

	F	S	M	B
U	CFU	CSU	CMU	
C	CFC	CSC	CMC	
R	CFR	CSR	CMR	
S	CFS	CSS	CMS	
T	CFT		CMT	
I	CFI		CMI	

"E" Evaluation

	F	S	M	B
U	EFU		EMU	
C				
R	EFR	ESR	EMR	
S	EFS		EMS	
T			EMT	
I	EFI			

"D" Divergent Production

	F	S	M	B
U		DSU	DMU	
C	DFC			
R			DMR	
S			DMS	
T		DST	DMT	
I			DMI	

"N" coNvergent Production

	F	S	M	B
U	NFU	NSU	NMU	
C	NFC		NMC	
R	NFR	NSR	NMR	
S	NFS	NSS	NMS	
T			NMT	
I	NFI	NSI	NMI	

F = Figural
S = Symbol
M = seMantic

U = Units
C = Classes
R = Relations
S = Systems
T = Transformation of material
I = Implication

1. Learning takes place first through cognition.
2. Storage of learned material is in memory.
3. Production of learned material may be:
   Unchanged = convergent "N" encoding or:
   Reoriented or invented = divergent "D" production.
4. One may or may not evaluate cognized (newly comprehended) material.

Note: Digits occasionally load on units, other times on systems. They may be scored in both cells.

* Adapted by Mary Meeker

FIGURE 9-2

BINET (LM) TEMPLATE FOR SOI ANALYSIS, YEARS II TO V

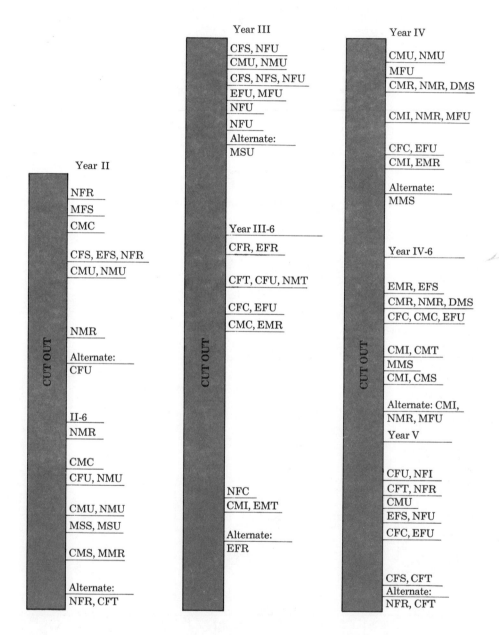

126

FIGURE 9-3

BINET (LM) TEMPLATE FOR SOI ANALYSIS, YEARS VI TO XI

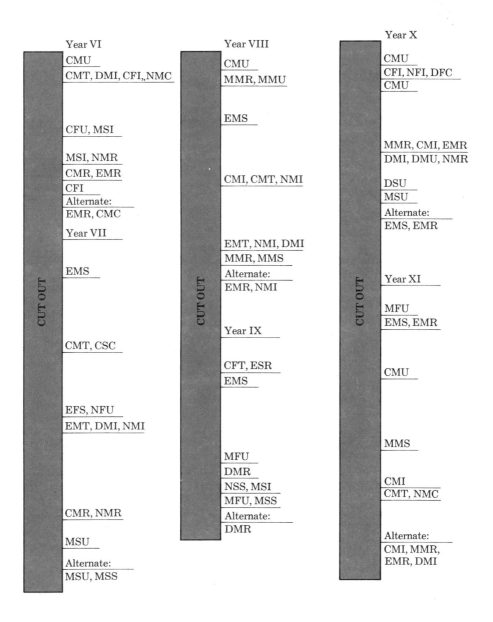

127

FIGURE 9-4

BINET (LM) TEMPLATE FOR SOI ANALYSIS, YEARS XII TO SAIII

CUT OUT

Year XII
CMU
EMR, EMS
EFI, EMS
MSS, MSU
CMU
CMR, EMR, NMI
Alternate: MFU
Year XIII
CFI
CMU
MMS
CMI, EMR
NMS, NMR
MFS, NFS
Alternate: CFT
Year XIV
CMU
CSS, NSR
MSS, NMI
CSC, DMT, NSI, DST
MFS, NFR, CFS
NMT
Alternate:
CSC, DMT, NSI, DST

CUT OUT

Average Adult
CMU
CSC, DMT, NSI, DST
CMU, EMU, CMR
CMS, MSI, NSS
CMI, NMT, DMS
MFS, NFR, CFS
CMU EMR, CMT
CMU
Alternate: CFT
Superior Adult I
CMU
MSS, MSI, MFT
CMR, EMR, NMI
MSS, MSU
CMU, DMR
CMT, NMT
Alternate: NMT

CUT OUT

Superior Adult II
CMU
MMR, CMI, EMR,
DMI, DMU, NMR
CMI, NMT, DMS
CSC, DMT, NSI, DST
CMU, EMR, CMT
MMR, CMS, NMU
Alternate:
CSR, CMR, NSR
Superior Adult III
CMU
CMI, NMT, DMS
CMR, CMU, NMR, DMU
MFS, NFR, CFS
NSS, MSI, ESR
MMR, CMS, NMU
Alternate:
CMR, CMU, NMU, DMU

TABLE 9-1

ACCUMULATED TOTALS* OF EXPECTED SCORE BY AGE LEVELS IN BINET LM FOR OPERATIONS IN THE SOI

+ Indicates Alternates

Year	Cognition	Memory	Evaluation	Convergent Production	Divergent Production
II	3^*+1	1	1	4	0
II-6	7+1	4	1	7+1	0
III	10	5+1	2	13	0
III-6	16	5	6+1	15	0
IV	21	7+1	8	18	1
IV-6	28+1	8+1	11	19+1	2
V	34+1	8	13	22+1	2
VI	40+1	10	14+1	24	3
VII	43	11+2	17	27	4
VIII	46	15	19+1	29+1	5
IX	47 49	19	21	30	6+1
X	51	21	22+2	32	10
XI	54+1	23+1	25+1	33	10+1
XII	57	25+1	30	34	10
XIII	60+1	27	31	37	10
XIV	64+1	29	31	42+1	12+2
AA	74+1	31	33	46	15
SAI	78	36	34	48+1	16
SAII	85+2	38	36	52+1	21
SAIII	91+2	41	37	57+1	23+1

If an alternate is given, add that number to the specific operation total for his mental age and subtract from each operation the factor count which would have been included in the item which was omitted for the alternate.

*Totals in each operation are exclusive of alternate items.

NOTE: This may be used as a gross operations score by counting successes on the flow diagram. Add the number correct in each operation and add to the total below the basal as indicated above.

TABLE 9-2

ACCUMULATED TOTALS* OF EXPECTED SCORE BY AGE LEVELS
IN BINET LM FOR CONTENTS IN THE SOI

+ Indicates Alternates

Year	Figural	Symbolic	Semantic
II	5^*+1	0	4
II-6	$6+2$	2	11
III	15	$2+1$	13
III-6	$22+1$	2	18
IV	26	2	$27+1$
IV-6	$29+1$	2	$37+2$
V	$39+2$	2	38
VI	42	4	$45+2$
VII	44	$6+2$	52
VIII	44	6	$64+2$
IX	47	10	$66+1$
X	50	12	$74+2$
XI	51	12	$82+4$
XII	$52+1$	14	90
XIII	$55+1$	14	96
XIV	58	$20+3$	$100+1$
AA	$61+1$	25	113
SAI	62	29	$121+1$
SAII	62	$32+2$	$138+1$
SAIII	65	35	$149+4$

If an alternate is given, add that number to the specific content total for his mental age and subtract from each content the factor count which would have been included in the item which was omitted for the alternate.

*Totals in each content are exclusive of alternate items.

NOTE: This may be used as a gross contents score by counting successes on the flow diagram. Add the number correct in each content and add to the total below the basal as indicated above.

TABLE 9-3

ACCUMULATED TOTALS OF EXPECTED SCORE BY AGE LEVELS
IN BINET LM FOR PRODUCTS IN THE SOI

+ Indicates Alternates

Year	Units	Classes	Relations	Systems	Transforma- tions	Implica- tions
II	2*+1	1	3	3	0	0
II-6	7	2	5+1	5	0+1	0
III	15+1	2	5	8	0	0
III-6	17	5	8+1	8	3	1
IV	22	6	12	9+1	3	3
IV-6	23+1	8	15+1	13	4	5+1
V	27	9	16+1	15	6+1	6
VI	29	10+1	19+1	15	7	11
VII	31+1	11	21	17+1	9	13
VIII	33	11	23+1	19	11	17+1
IX	35	11	25+1	22	12	18
X	40	12	28+1	22+1	12	22
XI	42	13	30+2	24	13	23+2
XII	45+1	13	33	27	13	25
XIII	46	13	35	31	13+1	27
XIV	47	14+1	37	35	16+2	29+1
AA	52	15	40	40	20+1	32
SAI	55	15	43	42	23+1	34
SAII	59	16	48+3	44	27	38
SAIII	63+3	16	53+1	49	28	40

If an alternate is given, add that number to the specific product total for his mental age and subtract from each product the factor count which would have been included in the item which was omitted for the alternate.

*Totals in each product are exclusive of alternate items.

NOTE: This may be used as a gross products score by counting successes on the flow diagram. Add the number correct in each product and add to the total below the basal as indicated above.

WISC

Materials Needed

1. 3 templates
2. A flow diagram of the SOI for each test administered
3. Chart showing expected number of factors for each age level
4. Profile for expected achievement accumulated by operations

Instructions: To analyze WISC for given SOI factors

1. Place template over WISC form.
2. Tally items correct from window in template. (Correct credit instructions are printed on each subtest template.)
3. Write tally number for the factor designated in the SOI Flow Diagram. Note: The correct factor cell is written in; number correct goes in the same box.

4. Compare items correct with expected achievement for age given in chart.

Interpretation: Look for pattern indications

1. Is he above or below his expected achievement?
2. Is any one of the five operations (cognition, memory, evaluation, convergent production, or divergent production) stronger or weaker than others? If so, how does this reflect his achievement in school?
3. Is he passing or failing in any horizontal dimension in one or more of the operations (units through implications)? Can the teacher orient curriculum toward his weakness or strength?
4. Is he passing or failing in any vertical direction? Is he strong in symbols but weak in semantics or vice versa? For example, if he is strong in symbols but weak in arithmetic, why? If he is poor in the semantic area, is it at the concrete (units) level only? At the implications level only? General weakness?

WPPSI

The WPPSI items are, for the most part, simply scaled down tests found in the WISC. Like the WISC, the WPPSI is a speed test where credit for correct answers is earned only when performed within the speed limits. The primary difference is the sub-test which incorporates Winterhaven and Bender-Gestalt types of visual-motor tasks. Because of this similarity, the instructions for using the templates are identical to those for using the WISC templates.

FIGURE 9-5
TALLY SHEET FOR WISC TEMPLATES

STRUCTURE OF INTELLECT
Flow Diagram of the Processes

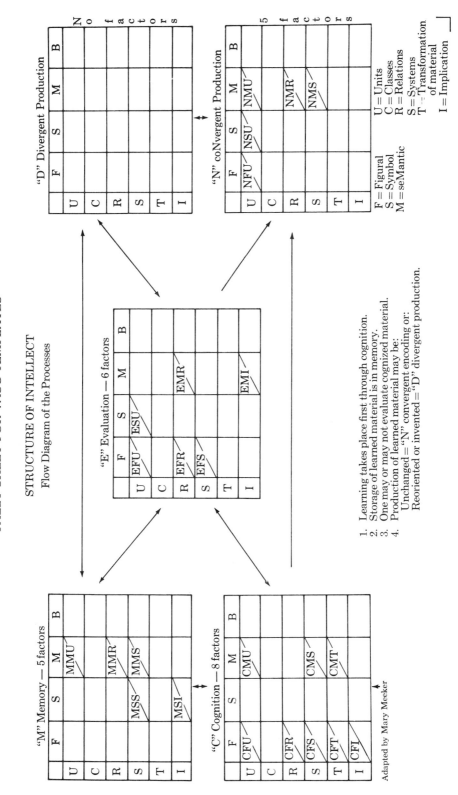

"D" Divergent Production

	F	S	M	B
U				
C				
R				
S				
T				
I				

No factors

"N" coNvergent Production

	F	S	M	B
U	NFU	NSU	NMU	
C				
R			NMR	
S			NMS	
T				
I				

5 factors

"E" Evaluation — 6 factors

	F	S	M	B
U	EFU	ESU		
C				
R	EFR		EMR	
S	EFS			
T				
I			EMI	

"M" Memory — 5 factors

	F	S	M	B
U			MMU	
C				
R			MMR	
S		MSS	MMS	
T				
I		MSI		

"C" Cognition — 8 factors

	F	S	M	B
U	CFU		CMU	
C				
R	CFR			
S	CFS		CMS	
T	CFT		CMT	
I	CFI			

U = Units
C = Classes
R = Relations
S = Systems
T = Transformation
      of material
I = Implication

F = Figural
S = Symbol
M = seMantic

1. Learning takes place first through cognition.
2. Storage of learned material is in memory.
3. One may or may not evaluate cognized material.
4. Production of learned material may be:
   Unchanged = "N" convergent encoding or:
   Reoriented or invented = "D" divergent production.

Adapted by Mary Meeker

133

FIGURE 9-6

WISC TEMPLATE FOR VERBAL TESTS, SUBTESTS 1, 2, 3

1. Information

1.	MMU						11.				CMU		21.				MSS	CMU	
2.	MMU						12.				CMU		22.						NMU
3.	MMU						13.	MMR					23.			MMR		CMU	
4.		MMR			EMR		14.	MMR		NMR			24.	MMU					NMU
5.		MMR					15.	MMR					25.	MMU					
6.					EMR		16.	MMR		NMR			26.			MMR			NMU
7.			MSS				17.	MMR		NMR			27.					CMU	
8.				MMS			18.				CMU		28.					CMU	
9.		MMR				NMR	19.		EMR				29.						NMU
10.			MSS				20.					NMU	30.					CMU	

Tally each factor for each item correct; some items have
two factors such as 4, 9, 14, 16, 17, 21, 23, 24, 26.

MMU _____
MMR _____
MSS _____
MMS _____
EMR _____
NMR _____
CMU _____
NMU _____

2. Comprehension

Note: credit is given for the ability (factor)
involved for each item, not the quality.

Tally total number of items correct
rather than the value of each to
get total of EMI factors.

EMI __8__

3. Arithmetic

Here each item
involves both
factors.

| Total items | 9 | MSI | CUT |
| correct each | 9 | CMS | CUT |

FIGURE 9-7

WISC TEMPLATE FOR VERBAL TESTS, SUBTESTS 4, 5, DIGITS AND MAZES

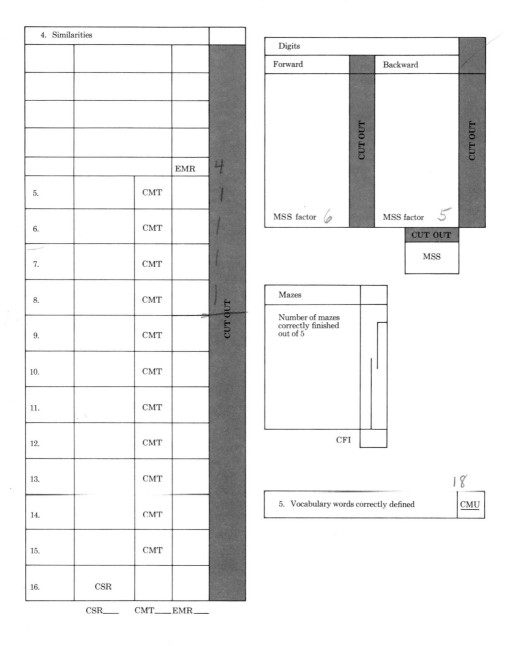

135

FIGURE 9-8

WISC TEMPLATE FOR VERBAL TESTS, SUBTESTS 6, 7, 8, 9, AND CODING

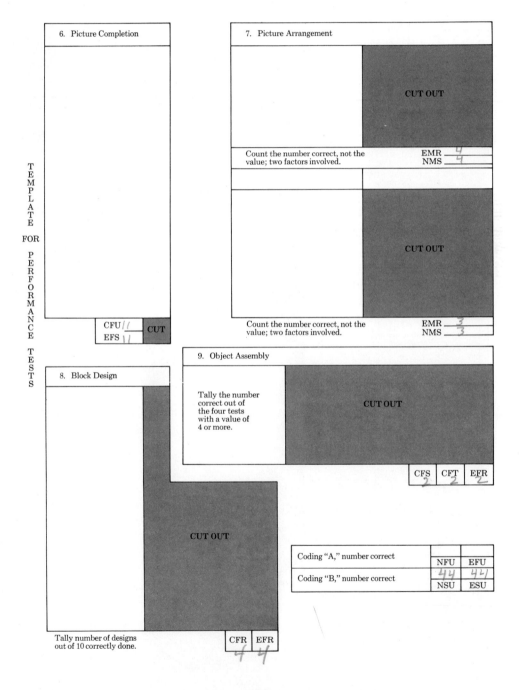

TEMPLATE FOR PERFORMANCE TESTS

6. Picture Completion

CFU // CUT

EFS ||

7. Picture Arrangement

CUT OUT

Count the number correct, not the value; two factors involved.

EMR ___ 4

NMS ___ 4

CUT OUT

Count the number correct, not the value; two factors involved.

EMR ___ 3

NMS ___ 3

9. Object Assembly

Tally the number correct out of the four tests with a value of 4 or more.

CUT OUT

CFS	CFT	EFR
2	2	2

8. Block Design

CUT OUT

Tally number of designs out of 10 correctly done.

CFR	EFR
4	4

Coding "A," number correct	NFU	EFU
Coding "B," number correct	44	44
	NSU	ESU

TABLE 9-4

SCALED EXPECTED FACTOR SCORE BY AGE FOR WISC

	Verbal Sub Tests								Compre-hension	Arithmetic		Similarities		Vocabu-lary	Digits: For-ward	Back-ward
	Information															
AGE	MMU	MMR	MSS	CMU	MMS	NMR	NMU	EMR	EMI	MSI	CMS	EMR	CMT	CMU	MSS	MSS
5.0-5.3	3	1						1	3	3	3	3		7	3	2
5.4-5.7	3	1						1	3	3	3	3		7	3	2
5.8-5.11	3	2						2	3	4	4	4	1	8	3	3
6.0-6.3	3	2						2	3	4	4	4		8	3	3
6.4-6.7	3	2						2	3	4	4	4		9	4	3
6.8-6.11	3	2		1				2	4	5	5	4	1	9	4	3
7.0-7.3	3	2	1	1				2	4	5	5	4	1	10	4	3
7.4-7.7	3	2	1	1				2	4	5	5	4	2	11	5	3
7.8-7.11	3	3	1	1		1		2	4	6	6	4	2	11	5	3
8.0-8.3	4	3	1	1	1	1		2	4	6	6	4	2	12	5	3
8.4-8.7	4	3	2	2	1	1		2	4	7	7	4	3	12	5	3
8.8-8.11	4	3	2	2	1	1		2	5	7	7	4	3	13	5	3
9.0-9.3	4	3	2	1	1	1		2	5	7	7	4	4	13	5	4
9.4-9.7	4	3	2	1	1	1		2	5	8	8	4	4	14	5	4
9.8-9.11	4	3	2	2	1	1		2	5	8	8	4	4	14	5	4
10.0-10.3	4	3	2	2	1	1		2	6	8	8	4	4	15	5	4
10.4-10.7	4	4	2	2	1	1		2	6	9	9	4	4	16	5	4
10.8-10.11	4	4	2	2	1	1		2	6	9	9	4	4	17	5	4
11.0-11.3	4	5	2	2	1	2		2	6	10	10	4	5	17	6	4
11.4-11.7	4	5	2	2	1	2		2	6	10	10	4	5	18	6	4
11.8-11.11	4	6	2	2	1	2		2	7	10	10	4	6	18	6	4
12.0-12.3	4	7	2	2	1	3		2	7	11	11	4	6	19	6	4
12.4-12.7	4	8	2	2	1	4		2	7	11	11	4	8	20	6	4
12.8-12.11	4	8	2	2	1	4		2	7	11	11	4	8	20	6	4
13.0-13.3	4	8	2	3	1	4		2	8	12	12	4	9	21	6	4
13.4-13.7	4	8	2	3	1	4		2	8	12	12	4	9	21	6	4
13.8-13.11	4	8	2	3	1	4		3	8	12	12	4	9	22	6	4
14.0-14.3	4	8	2	3	1	4		3	8	12	12	4	9	22	6	5
14.4-14.7	4	8	2	3	1	4		3	8	12	12	4	10	23	6	5
14.8-14.11	4	8	2	3	1	4		3	9	12	12	4	10	23	6	5
15.0-15.3	4	8	2	3	1	4		3	9	12	12	4	11	24	6	5
15.4-15.7	4	8	2	3	1	4		3	9	12	12	4	11	24	6	5
15.8-15.11	4	8	2	3	1	4	1	3	9	12	12	4	11	25	6	5

TABLE 9-5
SCALED EXPECTED AGE IN FACTORS FOR PERFORMANCE TESTS IN THE WISC

AGE	Picture Complet.		Picture Arr.		Block Design		Object Assembly			Coding		Mazes
	CFU	EFS	EMR	NMS	CFR	EFR	CFS	CFT	EFR	NFU	EFU	CFI
5.0-5.3	6	6			2	2	1	1	1	15	15	3
5.4-5.7	6	6	2	2	2	2	1	1	1	18	18	3
5.8-5.11	6	6	3	3	2	2	1	1	1	21	21	3
6.0-6.3	6	6	3	3	2	2	1	1	1	25	25	3
6.4-6.7	7	7	4	4	2	2	2	2	2	28	28	4
6.8-6.11	7	7	4	4	2	2	2	2	2	32	32	4
7.0-7.3	7	7	5	5	3	3	2	2	2	34	34	5
7.4-7.7	8	8	5	5	3	3	2	2	2	35	35	5
7.8-7.11	8	8	5	5	3	3	2	2	2	38	38	6
										NSU	ESU	
8.0-8.3	8	8	5	5	3	3	2	2	2	25	25	6
8.4-8.7	9	9	6	6	4	4	3	3	3	26	26	7
8.8-8.11	9	9	6	6	4	4	3	3	3	27	27	7
9.0-9.3	10	10	6	6	5	5	3	3	3	28	28	7
9.4-9.7	10	10	6	6	5	5	3	3	3	30	30	7
9.8-9.11	10	10	6	6	5	5	3	3	3	33	33	7
10.0-10.3	11	11	7	7	5	5	3	3	3	35	35	8
10.4-10.7	11	11	7	7	6	6	3	3	3	36	36	8
10.8-10.11	11	11	7	7	6	6	3	3	3	37	37	8
11.0-11.3	12	12	8	8	7	7	3	3	3	40	40	8
11.4-11.7	12	12	8	8	7	7	3	3	3	41	41	8
11.8-11.11	12	12	8	8	7	7	3	3	3	42	42	8
12.0-12.3	12	12	8	8	7	7	4	4	4	44	44	8
12.4-12.7	12	12	8	8	8	8	4	4	4	45	45	8
12.8-12.11	12	12	9	9	8	8	4	4	4	47	47	8
13.0-13.3	13	13	9	9	8	8	4	4	4	48	48	8
13.4-13.7	13	13	9	9	9	9	4	4	4	49	49	8
13.8-13.11	13	13	9	9	9	9	4	4	4	50	50	8
14.0-14.3	13	13	10	10	9	9	4	4	4	52	52	8
14.4-14.7	13	13	10	10	9	9	4	4	4	54	54	8
14.8-14.11	13	13	10	10	9	9	4	4	4	55	55	8
15.0-15.3	14	14	11	11	10	10	4	4	4	56	56	9
15.4-15.7	14	14	11	11	10	10	4	4	4	56	56	9
15.8-15.11	14	14	11	11	10	10	4	4	4	57	57	9

TABLE 9-6

ACCUMULATED TOTALS OF EXPECTED SCORES BY AGE LEVELS
FOR WISC OPERATIONS IN THE SOI

Year	Cognition	Memory	Evaluation	Convergent Production
End of Year				
5	22 + 3*	9 + 6**	42	24
6	28 + 4	11 + 7	57	36
7	34 + 6	14 + 8	66	44
			....code change	
8	43 + 7	17 + 8	60	34
9	49 + 7	18 + 9	68	40
10	55 + 8	20 + 9	76	45
11	61 + 8	23 + 10	85	52
12	70 + 8	26 + 10	94	60
13	76 + 8	27 + 10	100	63
14	78 + 8	27 + 11	107	66
15	83 + 9	27 + 11	112	73

*Add this number if mazes were used as a supplementary test; refer to scaled SOI for subtraction on any other test not given. Count separately.

**Add this number for combined forwards and backwards digits, if given.

Directions: Tabulate from scaled expectancy the expected score for the chronological age in the SOI profile. For example, in all of Cognition, total his successes and write this number over a diagonal like this — 9/ . Under the diagonal put the expected total for that operation. It may be 3+2+1. The total successes then would be 9/6. Count three beyond the chronological age and mark that point for each operation so tabulated.

Red line his chronological age across the accumulated totals as a reference line. The point of achievement in each operation thus marked will give a graph of his abilities in the operations.

FIGURE 9-9
TALLY SHEET FOR WPPSI TEMPLATES

Child's Name _____

I.Q. _____

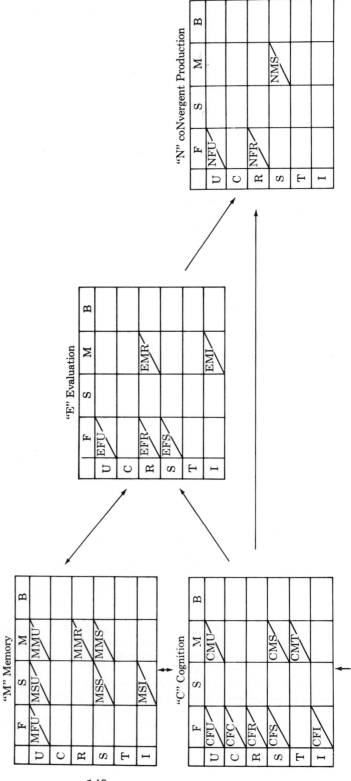

140

FIGURE 9-10

WPPSI TEMPLATE 1

Information		Animal House
	MMU	
	MMU	
	MMU	
	MMR EMR	
	MMR EMR	NFU EFU CUT
	MMU	
	CMU	Animal House Retest
	MMR EMR	
	MMR CMU	
	MFU CFS	
Tally each item to profile individually from here. Place number correct above diagonal ▱. Below diagonal place number he should have correct for his age as shown on scaled score.	EFU	NFU EFU CUT
	CMU	
	CFC CFR MMU	
	MMR EMR	
	EMR	
	MSS	
	EMR	
	MMS	
	EMR	
	CMU	
	CMU	
	MSS	
	MMR	

CUT OUT

Courtesy of Don Fraser

141

FIGURE 9-11

WPPSI TEMPLATE 2

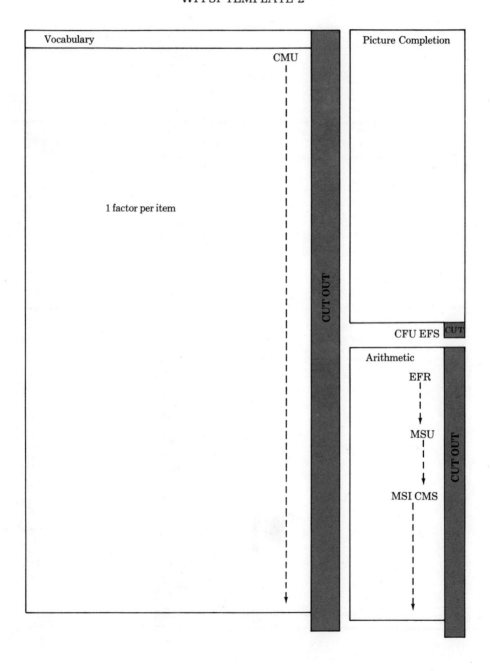

FIGURE 9-12

WPPSI TEMPLATE 3

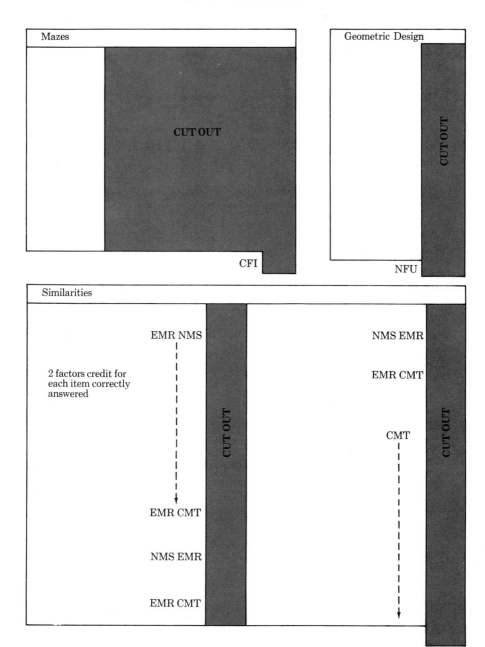

FIGURE 9-13

WPPSI TEMPLATE 4

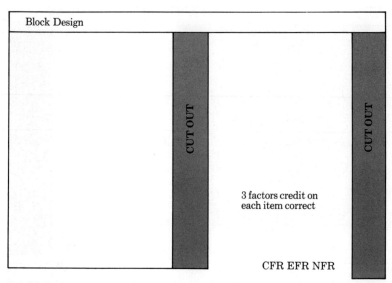

Block Design

CUT OUT

CUT OUT

3 factors credit on
each item correct

CFR EFR NFR

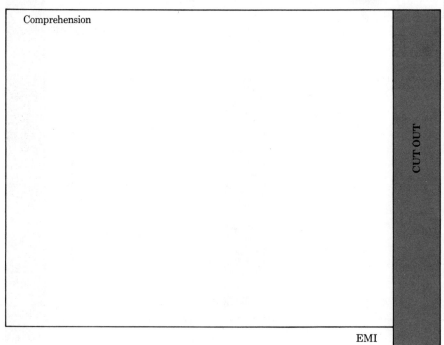

Comprehension

CUT OUT

EMI

FIGURE 9-14

WPPSI TEMPLATE 5

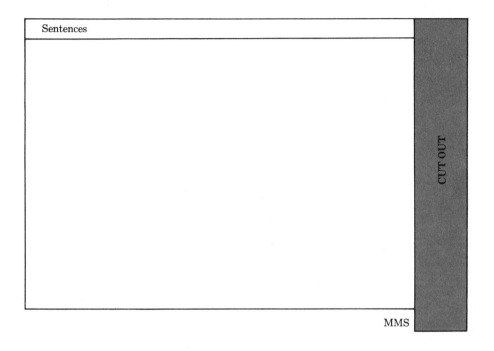

Sentences

CUT OUT

MMS

FIGURE 9-15
WPPSI TEMPLATE 6

Band 1

Age	Animal House NFU	Animal House EFU	Pict. Comp. CFU	Pict. Comp. EFS	Mazes CFI	Geo. De. NFU	Geo. De. CFR	Block Design EFR	Block Design NFR	Retest NFU	Retest EFU
4	17	17	6	6	2	2	2	2	2	24	24
4.25	21	21	7	7	3	2	3	3	3	31	31
4.5	27	27	9	9	4	2	3	3	3	38	38
4.75	32	32	10	10	5	3	4	4	4	42	42
5	36	36	11	11	6	4	4	4	4	45	45
5.25	39	39	12	12	7	4	5	5	5	48	48
5.5	45	45	13	13	7	5	6	6	6	51	51
5.75	48	48	13	13	7	6	6	6	6	53	53
6	51	51	14	14	8	6	7	7	7	54	54
6.25	53	53	15	15	8	6	7	7	7	56	56
6.5	55	55	16	16	8	7	8	8	8	57	57

Band 2

Age	MMU	MMR	EMR	CMU	Information CFS	Information EFU	Similarities NMS	CFC	CFR	Retest MSS	Retest MFU	Comp. EMI	Sent. MMS
4	4	2	2	1			5					3	5
4.25	4	3	3	1			5					3	6
4.5	4	4	3	2	1		6				1	4	6
4.75	4	4	3	2	1	1	6				1	4	7
5	4	4	3	3	1	1	7		1		1	5	7
5.25	5	4	3	3	1	1	7	1	1		1	5	8
5.5	5	5	3	3	1	1	7	1	1		1	5	8
5.75	5	5	4	3	1	1	7	1	1		1	6	9
6	5	5	4	3	1	1	7	1	1	1	1	6	9
6.25	5	5	5	3	1	1	7	1	1		1	7	10
6.5	5	5	5	3	1	1	7	1	1		1	7	10

Band 3

Age	Vocab. CMU	EFR	Arithmetic MSU	Arithmetic MSI	Information CMS	Information EMR	CMT
4	5	4	1	1	1	5	1
4.25	6	4	2	1	1	6	1
4.5	7	4	3	2	2	7	2
4.75	7	4	4	3	3	8	2
5	8	4	4	4	3	9	2
5.25	8	4	4	4	4	9	3
5.5	9	4	4	5	5	10	4
5.75	9	4	4	6	6	10	5
6	10	4	4			10	6
6.25	10	4	4			10	7
6.5	11	4	4			10	

10

Automated Programming Based on SOI Profiles

The school psychologists' findings need no longer end with the placing of an IQ score behind a pupil's name. What do the components of that IQ mean? How can they be related to his needs in curriculum practice? What is the best way to communicate the psychological findings to the teacher who must use them?

When the Binet responses have been plotted into the SOI Flow Diagram, the diagram becomes a profile of that child's intellectual abilities. It is not the kind of profile, however, which can be used easily as a teaching tool. It is complex, difficult to interpret, and difficult to relate to curriculum practices. Although the procedure of plotting the responses takes only a few minutes, the understanding of the SOI takes more time and requires in-service training.

Communication for teacher usefulness remained a problem until, with the cooperation of the Redondo Beach (California) School Psychologists, the idea of automated programming was explored. Psychologists know that the detailed writing of summaries of findings and recommendations of any kind occupies so much of their time that it takes them away from screening, testing, and consulting with teachers and parents. Yet they believe that these latter duties are of equal importance in their work. With the development of automated individual programs, we did not want to infringe upon the teacher's creativity or to spoon-feed her the results. We wanted her to use it as a model for planning.

We developed a form which finally met our criteria. Examples of this form are shown on the following pages (tables 10-1, 10-2, 10-3, 10-4). The forms proved to be useful for reporting findings from the ITPA, sensori-motor tests, and SOI analyses.

TABLE 10-1

FORMAT FOR INDIVIDUALIZATION OF TEACHING

Name: Girl

CA =7- 5	CAGP=2.2
MA=6-10	MAGP=1.7
	AGP=2.2

Objective or Goal: (MSU) — Memory of letters and numbers, deficit

Other Disabilities: Memory of symbols, involving both auditory (CA=4-2) and visual (CA=5-4) channels

RECOMMENDATIONS TO TEACHER

Materials:	General:
Beads Visual figures Digits and letters (written, auditory, plastic) Oral directions (teacher or tape recorder) Pictures of bead designs Language Master	Use Language Master to extend time between repetition of digits and letters. Assignments need to be short, and practice distributed. Use rewards as reinforcement.
	Specific: 1. a. Copy bead sequences watching model. b. Copy bead sequences from memory. 2. Recall visual and auditory series of digits and letters. 3. Recall visual figural patterns. 4. Relearn #2 and #3. 5. Follow oral directions.
	Testing for Learning: Amount of time saved in relearning Degree of correctness in recall Success in following directions Overlearning, repetition
	Reinforcement: Check marks Stars Record card (feedback) "Good" Record of successes (plus feedback) Schedule of reinforcement should be continuous at first and then lower ratio (1:3).

TABLE 10-2

FORMAT FOR INDIVIDUALIZATION OF TEACHING

Name: Girl

CA = 7- 5	CAGP = 2.2
MA = 6-10	MAGP = 1.7
	AGP = 2.2

Objective or Goal (CFU) (CSC) (CSS) — Develop perception of units by classifying

Disabilities: Audio and visual memory
Sequencing
Units (figural, symbolic, semantic)

Strengths: Figural, divergency, implications

RECOMMENDATIONS TO TEACHER

Materials: Magazines and pictures Colored paper and paste Crayon and pencil	**CSC** Ask her to impose her own way of classifying in terms of families or how alike.
Observable Responses: Watch for perseveration at end of week	**CFU** Let her learn to perceive units by having her classify pictures. This will lead to her establishing relations within her own system of classifications.
	CSS Teacher will write child's classification under the picture using the child's words.
	CSS After several systems have been classified, have her break them apart and re-classify on a different basis.
	Reinforcement: Star, candy, or name on board for each classification

149

TABLE 10-3

FORMAT FOR INDIVIDUALIZATION OF TEACHING

Name: Girl

CA =7- 5	CAGP=2.2
MA=6-10	MAGP=1.7
	AGP=2.2

Objective or Goal: (CMU) — Expression of ideas in words (Vocal Encoding) — vocabulary

Disabilities: Inadequate verbal fluency and inability to express ideas in spoken words (CA=5-1)

RECOMMENDATIONS TO TEACHER

Materials:	
Concrete objects (e.g., chair, window)	Alternate activities
	Materials must be based on interests.
Pictures	Describe simple objects.
Story record	Describe pictures.
Incomplete sentences (vocal presentation)	Sentence completion (vocally)
	Tell story with puppets.
Puppets	Tell story about cartoons.
Cartoons	Share past experiences.
Sharing time	Teacher and/or group listen to girl speak.
	Tape record some verbal output.
	Reinforcement:
	Attitude of teacher
	Verbal praise
	Recognition
	Response of others
	Affection (pat or hug)
	Verbal praise ("good")
	Responding to verbalizations (teacher, pupils)
	Continuous reinforcement schedule
	Receptive accepting attitude

Of the 22 teachers involved in the Redondo Beach learning disabilities classes, nearly all felt that the structuring of the disabilities allowed them to work with individual rates of learning, that the formats saved them time in lesson planning and although the goals were not the kinds they had ever made educational plans for before, they nevertheless enjoyed finding materials to use for the achievement of these goals. Harry McKee, chief psychologist for the Redondo Beach Elementary Schools, reported that plans for a two-year evaluation study were in progress.

TABLE 10-4

FORMAT FOR INDIVIDUALIZATION OF TEACHING

Name: Girl

CA =7- 5   CAGP=2.2
MA=6-10   MAGP=1.7
AGP=2.2

Objective or Goal: (EFU) — Figure-ground perception

RECOMMENDATIONS TO TEACHER

Materials:	
Variety of objects in box	Ask her to pick out particular objects from the box of many objects. At first objects should differ greatly, later minimal differences.
	Learn to concentrate on specific stimuli. After success has been reached in terms of concrete objects, teacher can shift to pictures utilizing the same process. Observable Responses: Training in figure-ground perception should result in improved ability to shift attention appropriately, to concentrate on relevant stimuli and ignore irrelevant stimuli.
	Reinforcement: Stars, candy or name on board When pictures are successfully mastered, teacher will write child's word for objects. Reinforcement for successful picture named and reward for recognition of reading word.

The forms shown here have been filled in with data collected on one child.

Common Abilities in the Binet and WISC

Psychologists who use the SOI analyses for the first time frequently ask whether or not there are confirmations of findings from one test to another. Mr. Lewis Phillips of the University of British Columbia developed a graph to show these commonalities for one student.

Figure 10-1 shows the cell assignations from the Binet LM, WISC, and ITPA. All three of these tests were administered to an eight-year-old student who was considered to be "bright" by his teacher but who was not reading well. The Binet IQ score was 120; the WISC Verbal was 95; the

FIGURE 10-1

CELL ASSIGNATIONS FROM THE BINET-LM, WISC, AND ITPA

```
C.A.                8.4
I.Q. — Binet        120
        WISC   V-95      } 91
               P-87
Goodenough —        77
```

Binet — WISC — ITPA: Plotted on one graph to show Strengths and Weaknesses common in test scores by subject

	Figural		Symbolic		seMantic	
Units M C E D N						
Classes M C E D N						
Relations M C E D N						
Systems M C E D N	+W					
Transformation M C E D N			+B			
Implications M C E D N	+B	+B		+W / +B		

Weaknesses
Binet ▆▆▆
WISC ▨▨▨
ITPA ⣿⣿

Strengths
Binet +B
WISC +W
ITPA +I

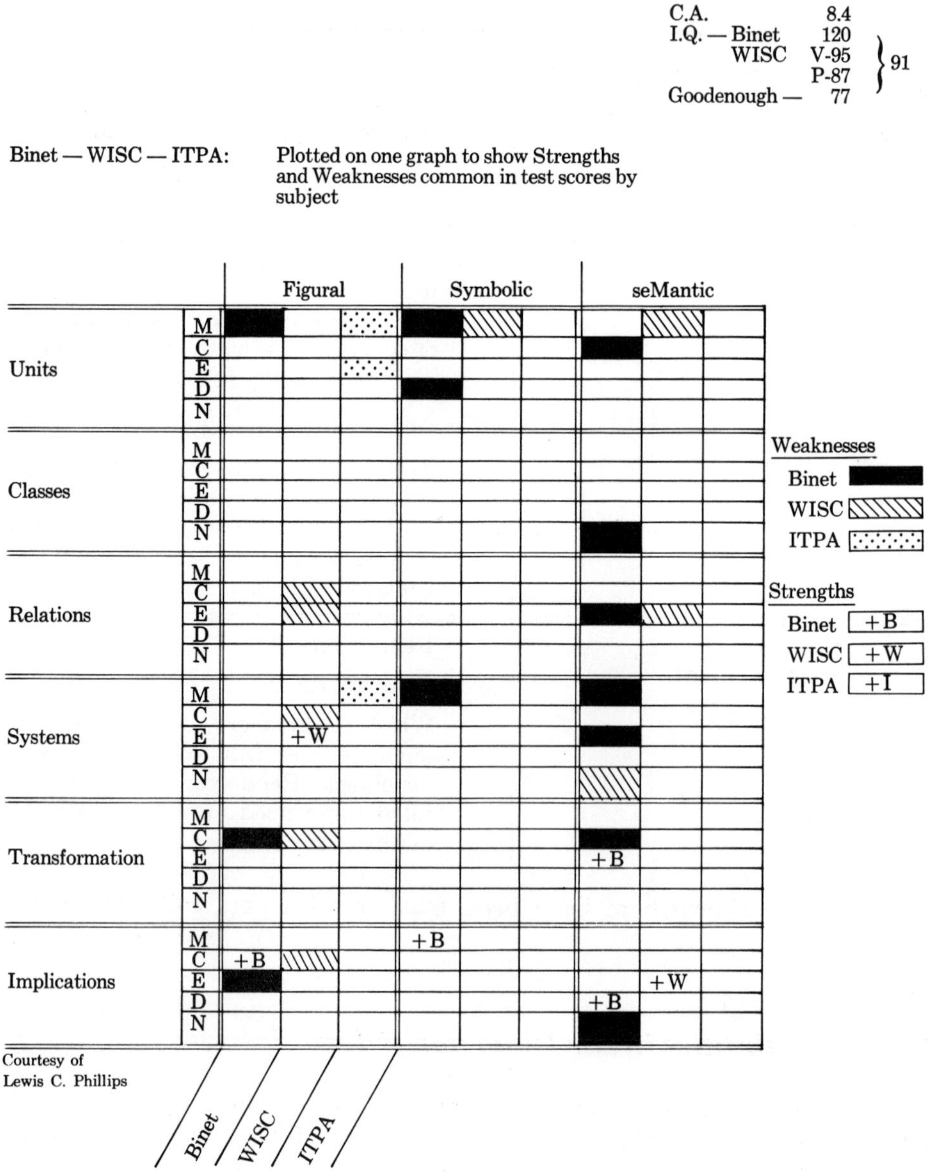

Courtesy of
Lewis C. Phillips

Binet   WISC   ITPA

WISC Performance was 87, giving a total IQ score of 91. The Goodenough Draw-A-Person revealed a mental-age projected IQ score of 77.

Figure 10-1 was plotted to show the common strengths and weaknesses found in one subject's scores on a battery of tests. The child had superior intelligence but was unable to perform visual motor coordination tasks most children his age could perform; it was suspected that there was perceptual dysfunctioning. All three tests showed deficits in the units dimension across memory, evaluation, cognition and divergent production. Cognition and decoding (ITPA) abilities were good. Both the WISC and Binet showed common weakness in the relations dimension for evaluation; both the Binet and WISC showed common strengths in implications abilities across operations and contents.

Since three tests showed deficits in the units dimension, there were concerns about his ability to learn to read even though his IQ score was good. Other SOI profiles showing similar patterns of deficits in discriminating and recalling units have been found to be associated with reading problems; in fact, deficits in memory most frequently are associated with academic retardation regardless of the IQ score. As a consequence of the psychometric findings, the child was given specific training in visual-motor skills and referred for medical examination. Appropriate academic expectations were discussed with the parents and teacher.

Investigations into specific relationships of certain SOI factors to prereading and later reading success skills are currently underway for a doctoral dissertation by B. Feldman at the University of Southern California, Los Angeles.

11

SOI Profiles
for Clinical Types

This chapter consists of a series of SOI profiles and interpretations. Several profiles come from matched IQ scores and are presented to show the differences in intellectual patterns.

There are some generalizations which can be made now about clinical groups or school types; these generalizations are based on reading and interpreting over a thousand profiles on children in the United States and Canada.

1. *Gifted children, normal IQ scoring children,* and *mental retardates* of a type all show similar patterns. That is, there are no "group" characteristics. There will be individual patterns with strengths and weaknesses in any one of the three dimensions. They may be weak, strong or average in any one of the operations. Another dimension, contents, will show almost any kind of patterning, as will products.

2. *Educationally handicapped children* (defined as children with IQ scores of 90 or more who are two or more years retarded in academic achievement as measured by group or individual achievement tests) show a group pattern. They may have individual strengths or weaknesses in any dimension, but they show a common weakness in memory items.

3. Hayes-Binets on *blind-from-birth children* also show inter-group patterns. Those who score below 140 show deficits in figural items across operations and in relations items. Blind children (to age 17) with IQ's over 140 do not show deficits in figural and relations items, but rather show individual patterns similar to other gifted students.

4. Boys with *social problems* who have been classed as *incorrigible* show deficits in evaluation.

5. *Highly anxious students* tend to do poorly in divergent-production items; however, this is a trend and does not always hold true. Anxiety has typically been ascertained by clinical insight rather than by measuring instruments alone.

Individual Profiles Based on SOI Analyses

This section shows profiles of several clinical types of students. Their Binet or WISC responses form SOI patterns which make available to the psychologist more information than is usually reported in the traditional score and summary.

The following profiles show how the Binet and WISC look when they have been mapped into an SOI profile. The procedure of getting test responses into an SOI profile is a simple tabulation from the templates to the flow diagram, taking up to five minutes, and is described more accurately in another section. Color coding the Binet responses is not necessary but is helpful in making basal and ceiling responses more obvious.

Because the WISC is a spiral test, an additional step in tabulation is required; the psychologist must turn to the scaled scores to get a normative level. A diagonal line is used on the SOI profile to cut the trigraph cell in half. The number of correct factor responses are placed above the diagonal like a numerator. The number appearing below the diagonal (like a denominator) is taken from the scaled score which shows the number of correct responses the examinee should have made for his age. The factor counts were taken from the scaled scores for IQ scores of 100 at each age level shown.

WISC Profiles

Since the WISC requires this more complex procedure, the first profile (FIG. 11-1) to be shown is that of a boy with a WISC IQ of 80.

He was ten and had been in EMR classes for three years. The school psychologist and teacher both felt strongly that he was not a typical retardate. The first test for placement gave him an IQ score of 68. The test shown here, with a WISC IQ score of 80, was his re-evaluation. Both first and second tests were placed into SOI profiles and showed similar patterns. The responses show that in cognition and in memory he is average or above. Since his failures are clearly in the evaluation and convergent-production areas, they were interpreted as encoding types of performance problems. It was suspected that he was minimally brain damaged rather than a typical EMR. This profile also differed markedly from other EMR profiles which usually show cell strengths and weaknesses in a more scattered fashion.

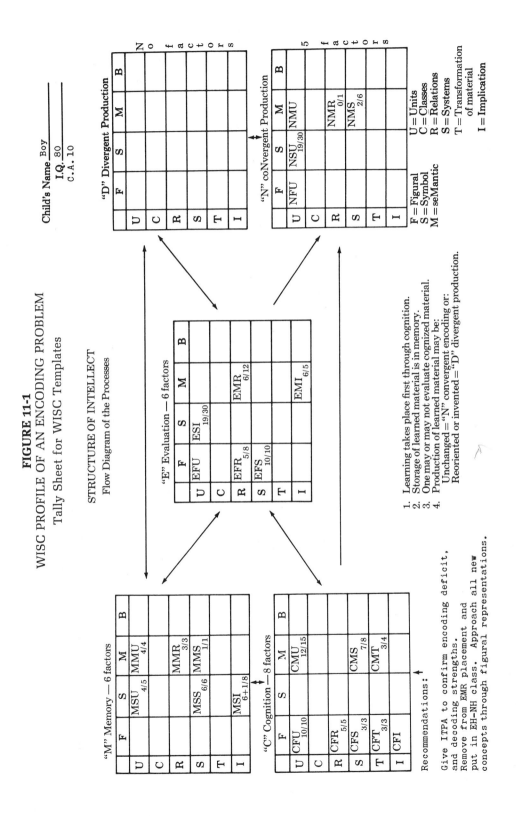

FIGURE 11-1
WISC PROFILE OF AN ENCODING PROBLEM
Tally Sheet for WISC Templates

STRUCTURE OF INTELLECT
Flow Diagram of the Processes

Child's Name Boy
I.Q. 80
C.A. 10

1. Learning takes place first through cognition.
2. Storage of learned material is in memory.
3. One may or may not evaluate cognized material.
4. Production of learned material may be:
   Unchanged = "N" convergent encoding or:
   Reoriented or invented = "D" divergent production.

Recommendations:

Give ITPA to confirm encoding deficit, and decoding strengths. Remove from EMR placement and put in EH-NH class. Approach all new concepts through figural representations.

F = Figural
S = Symbol
M = seMantic

U = Units
C = Classes
R = Relations
S = Systems
T = Transformation of material
I = Implication

The first classes for educationally handicapped had just begun in this district. Based on the SOI and ITPA findings, it was decided to place this boy in an EH class, and remove him from the EMR grouping. In the EH class he was given individualized curriculum based on the SOI findings. He was also taught new concepts first through figural or concrete representations. His progress was slow but steady for a period of two years. He is now in a regular classroom, in a lower group; but on the basis of his progress, it was determined that the original diagnosis of EMR had been incorrect. An exact description of classroom facilities for educationally handicapped classes can be read in the Special Child Publications, *Educational Therapy II*, 1968, "An Evaluation of the Educationally Handicapped Program After Two Years: The Measurables and the Unmeasurables."

A second boy, whose profile was not available for publication, but who had higher decoding and cognition abilities, a Peabody Picture Vocabulary score of 136 and a Binet score of 60, was also placed in the EH class where booths, SOI programming, teaching machines, and the Language Master were used. This boy, at the end of two years, was returned to normal classes and is still functioning at and above grade level in various subjects.

Binet Profiles

A boy in the fourth grade (FIG. 11-2), had been retained once and the school had recommended retention for the second time. The boy was so upset about another retention that his mother sought outside help. She felt he was very bright and something else was wrong.

His Binet was high, and Wide Range Achievement Tests placed him at the seventh-grade level, except in spelling, which was low, yet he was unable to keep up with his work. He was not a real discipline problem, but the teachers felt he frequently showed poor judgment and could not be depended on to work independently or adequately, yet his verbal ability was so superior that he posed an enigma. (Note the strength in the "M", seMantic, columns except in evaluation.) His auditory problem solving in math was very high and when he was called on in class, he could be depended on to come up with correct answers in verbal solutions, although his written work was poor. (Note strengths in symbols. The Binet, it must be remembered, is essentially an auditory test.)

The only SOI weaknesses were his failures in figural items, and this was a small sampling. School records showed two normal visual examinations, nevertheless we requested an orthoptics examination because of the figural and spelling deficits. The examination showed a most unusual visual defect, and corrective glasses were provided. On the basis of his high IQ score, the school principal agreed to let him go on with his class. Improvement was immediate in all written work, but especially so in spelling; in fact, he was soon taking "bonus" words in a month and making A's repeatedly. Similar results occurred in written math. His motivation was, of course, very high, as visual learning became easy.

FIGURE 11-2
BINET PROFILE OF A SUPERIOR STUDENT WITH FIGURAL PROBLEMS
Tally Sheet for Stanford-Binet (LM) Templates

Child's Name ___Male___
I.Q. ___superior___

STRUCTURE OF INTELLECT PROFILE
With a Flow Diagram of the Processes

"M" Memory

	F	S	M	B
U	MFU +	MSU +	MMU	
C				
R			MMR	
S	MFS -	MSS +	MMS -+	
T	MFT			
I		MSI +		

6/9

"C" Cognition

	F	S	M	B
U	CFU		CMU ++++-	
C	CFC	CSC	CMC	
R	CFR	CSR ++	CMR +	
S	CFS -	CSS +	CMS +	
T	CFT		CMT +	
I	CFI -		CMI ++	

12/15

Basal	11
Year	12
	13
	14
	AA

"E" Evaluation

	F	S	M	B
U	EFU			
C				
R	EFR	ESR	EMR -+++	
S	EFS		EMS +--	
T			EMT	
I	EFI -			

5/9

"D" Divergent Production

	F	S	M	B
U		DSU	DMU	
C	DFC			
R			DMR	
S			DMS	
T		DST +	DMT +	
I			DMI	

2/2

"N" coNvergent Production

	F	S	M	B
U	NFU		NMU	
C	NFC		NMC +	
R	NFR -	NSR +	NMR	
S	NFS	NSS	NMS +	
T			NMT +	
I	NFI +	NSI +	NMI +++	

9/10

U = Units
C = Classes
R = Relations
S = Systems
T = Transformation of material
I = Implication

F = Figural
S = Symbol
M = seMantic

1. Learning takes place first through cognition.
2. Storage of learned material is in memory.
3. Production of learned material may be:
   Unchanged = convergent "N" encoding or:
   Reoriented or invented = divergent "D" production.
4. One may or may not evaluate cognized (newly comprehended) material.

The patterns for these profiles (FIGURES 11-1 to 11-15) are self-explanatory and were selected so that color coding would not be essential; however, in practice, the psychologist might want to use different colors for basal and ceiling references.

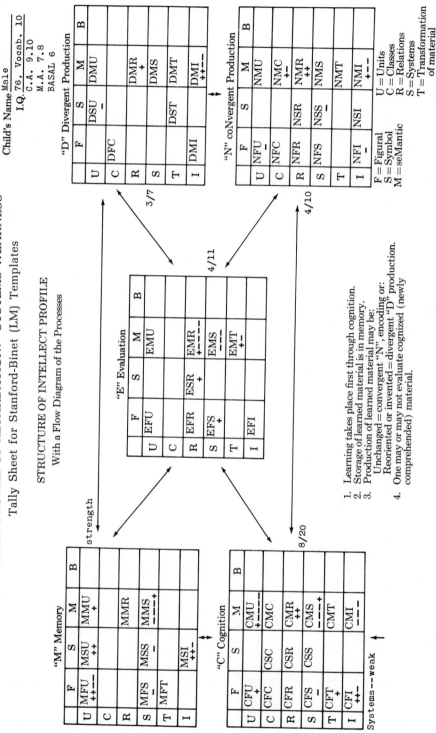

FIGURE 11-3

BINET PROFILE OF RETARDATION: SYSTEMS WEAKNESS

Tally Sheet for Stanford-Binet (LM) Templates

STRUCTURE OF INTELLECT PROFILE

With a Flow Diagram of the Processes

Child's Name __Male__

I.Q. 76, Vocab. 10
C.A. 9.10
M.A. 7.8
BASAL 6

strength

Systems--weak

1. Learning takes place first through cognition.
2. Storage of learned material is in memory.
3. Production of learned material may be:
   Unchanged = convergent "N", encoding or:
   Reoriented or invented = divergent "D" production.
4. One may or may not evaluate cognized (newly comprehended) material.

F = Figural
S = Symbol
M = seMantic

U = Units
C = Classes
R = Relations
S = Systems
T = Transformation
      of material
I = Implication

FIGURE 11-4

BINET PROFILE OF RETARDATION: DECODING STRENGTHS

Tally Sheet for Stanford-Binet (LM) Templates

STRUCTURE OF INTELLECT PROFILE
With a Flow Diagram of the Processes

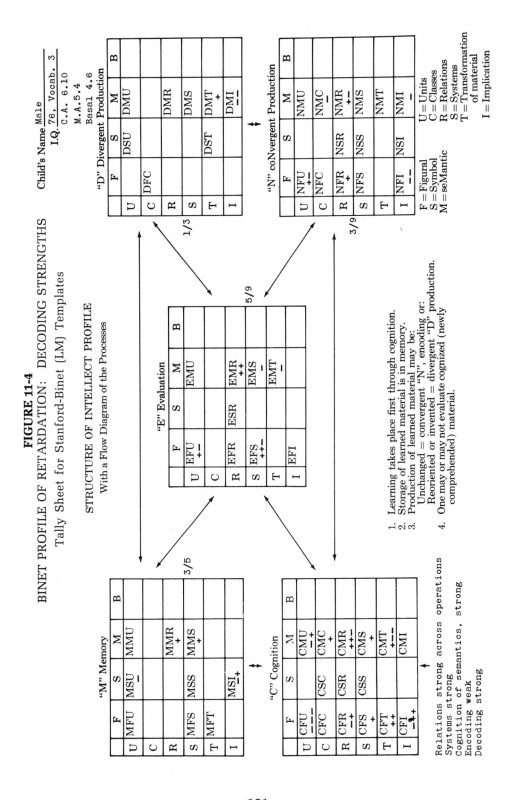

Child's Name Male

I.Q. 76, Vocab. 3

C.A. 6.10

M.A.5.4

Basal 4.6

"D" Divergent Production

	F	S	M	B
U		DSU	DMU	
C	DFC			
R			DMR	
S			DMS	
T		DST	DMT +	
I			DMI −	

1/3

"N" coNvergent Production

	F	S	M	B
U	NFU +−	NSR	NMU	
C	NFC		NMC	
R	NFR +	NSR	NMR +−	
S	NFS	NSS	NMS	
T			NMT	
I	NFI −−	NSI	NMI −	

3/9

F = Figural
S = Symbol
M = seMantic

U = Units
C = Classes
R = Relations
S = Systems
T = Transformation
    of material
I = Implication

"E" Evaluation

	F	S	M	B
U	EFU +−		EMU	
C				
R	EFR	ESR	EMR ++	
S	EFS ++		EMS −	
T			EMT −	
I	EFI			

5/9

"M" Memory

	F	S	M	B
U	MFU	MSU −	MMU	
C				
R			MMR +	
S	MFS	MSS	MMS +	
T	MFT			
I		MSI −+		

3/5

"C" Cognition

	F	S	M	B
U	CFU −−		CMU −+	
C	CFC	CSC	CMC +	
R	CFR −+	CSR	CMR ++−	
S	CFS +	CSS	CMS +	
T	CFT ++		CMT −−	
I	CFI −+		CMI	

Relations strong across operations
Systems strong
Cognition of semantics, strong
Encoding weak
Decoding strong

1. Learning takes place first through cognition.
2. Storage of learned material is in memory.
3. Production of learned material may be:
   Unchanged = convergent "N", encoding or:
   Reoriented or invented = divergent "D" production.
4. One may or may not evaluate cognized (newly
   comprehended) material.

161

Evaluation and judgment exercises were prescribed which parents were able to render. We asked his teacher to give him problem situations which depended on talking out alternate decisions, and to give him practice in committee leadership where he would have to make judgments. We felt sure his academic success would continue, and it has.

Mentally Retarded Children.   Figures 11-3 and 11-4 are two profiles of boys who have been placed in the same class for educable mental retardates.

Figure 11-3 shows the following individual differences in a pattern of a typical MR whose IQ score was 76.

1)   A look at the individual major operation blocks indicates that a count of proportions of successes to failures shows no particular strengths unless it is memory for units. There is a weakness in CMU, vocabulary. He got about half of each of the total responses correct. Memory is his strongest operation, thus we can assume some associative abilities to be intact.

2)   Next we will check the figural columns. The decoding of figures shows some strength (C and M), but encoding figural items is weak. Out of three possible items, he got none correct. In view of the usual approach for mental retardates — exposing them to concrete objects first — he can grasp such material, but if he is tested or expected to perform successfully, this pattern shows that he would fail to measure up to such expectations.

3)   Looking at symbolic responses, memory for symbols shows strength; but encoding (N and D) symbols, however, show weakness; the one response in evaluation was a success.

4)   Looking at semantics, we see a preponderance of failures in cognition, memory, and evaluation, but proportionately more successes in semantic items where production or encoding is required.

5)   To examine the horizontal dimension, products, we look at units, across the five operations. We see some strength in memory; other responses are not so strong.

There are too few responses in classes. Relations, however, show that out of 11 responses (three at ceiling), he got eight correct. The teacher can depend on his ability to see relations at his level, and this will be her clue for an individual approach for teaching him — approaching him through his strengths. With his difficulty in encoding or producing, he will have to be shown the relationships for each bit of information he is given. That is, he should be taught by "bits," and in each instance he should be shown how this "bit" is related to the next and to preceding material. We see weakness in "C" cognizing and "N" convergent production of implications (I) in words (M). A weakness in systems (S) in evaluation, alerts us to the fact that such a pattern, coupled with the semantic weakness, might well predict difficulty in judgment and perception of semantic systems which, if occurring in the social area, will eventuate in behavior problems in the school room or on the playground. This was, in fact, the case reported by the teacher. She said that this boy was most troublesome and generally did not seem to understand cause and effect. She literally had to keep him by the hand. With the weakness in semantic relations combined with semantic systems weakness in evaluation, it is possible to understand how these deficits cause difficulties for the child.

A program based on his individual pattern of abilities would consist of the following.

1. Approach any new learning task through figural or tactile modes. Try to demonstrate relations between any concrete object or figural representation and its visual representation; that is, build up associations.

2. In spelling, for instance, a picture or an object of the word must appear with the word.

3. Repetition of simple bits of information is necessary for him to grasp the material. Use a conditioning approach in numerals or words when presented.

4. With the weaknesses in implications and semantics, a total program for him should exclude as much as possible emphasis on such tasks.

5. Vocational training in which he handles the materials would be more successful and more to his liking. Vocational considerations should begin early.

Figure 11-4 shows responses of a boy with the same IQ score. His pattern indicates strength in cognition, particularly in semantics and implications. This is in contrast with those of Figure 11-3. Implications in the productions are poor and the productions generally are weak. Memory, on the other hand, shows more strengths at the units and implications levels, although cognition of units is poor. Relations are strong across operations, and so are systems. One can, on the basis of this profile, expect greater comprehension of abstract concepts, and his program could well include more semantic training. Both boys need experiences and training in evaluative situations and specifically in those situations where they will be called upon to make judgments related to personal safety.

The process whereby we explode an IQ score enables us to determine whether the student's intellectual deficits and strengths are those of a decoding or encoding nature.

This process, gross as it presently is, is enough of a refinement to separate mentally retarded patterns into more reasonable categories. That is, although the IQ score may indicate mental retardation, if there is a pattern in the SOI of deficits solely in the encoding (convergent- or divergent-production areas) or decoding (cognition and some aspects of evaluation), the probability is that the child is a functional retardate, and we can then consider the possibility that a brain damage of some type has occurred. Particularly is this so when an ITPA profile confirms the SOI analytic findings, or when the Bender-Gestalt is not that of a typical retardate.

This separation of types of retardation is important because it means different curricular treatments and differing expectations for the child's future. It is especially relevant to the mental health of the parents and the child. It is specifically desirable in planning for the child's future as an independent citizen.

There are ways, however, to refine even these diagnoses more. Two ways in which this can be done consist of medical procedures. One is well established and expensive — that is a chromosonal count. The other is new, experimental, very exciting and promising, because it is quick, easy, inexpensive, and may prove to be a physical correlate to a mental condition. It is the fingernail-bed capillary microscopy (Higashino and Moss, 1967) study which has shown, at least experimentally, that poorly shaped capillaries typify mongolism, cystic fibrosis, and congenital heart conditions.

Figure 11-5 shows the Binet-SOI responses of a ten-year-old boy whose IQ was 55. He had been in public school in regular classes until he began fighting and became uncontrollable at home and at school. The father reported that the boy's temper would flare up suddenly, and that the hostility and aggressiveness frightened others because the boy was so strong. He was tall, rather heavy, and an alert-looking boy who could understand many things which made him seem older and sophisticated for his age. Yet he could neither count nor work with numbers. He could repeat the alphabet, but he could not identify the letters out of context. He could write his name and draw fairly well. Clinical impressions of two psychologists were such that they hesitated about labeling this as simple retardation.

The responses on the SOI profile (FIG. 11-5) showed real strengths in all figural items across operations, and fairly good cognition. Short-term and long-term memory were weak, so the obvious failures in the associative area and the encoding of semantics led to a hypothesis that perhaps this was a brain damage of some kind, reflected in semantic encoding problems. There was a history of difficult labor and forceps delivery.

The school district and home environment were such that a choice of institutional placement or private school placement had to be made. In the meantime, it was decided to have a capillary microscopic study made (Higashino and Moss, 1967) at the UCLA medical school to see whether the capillaries were of the normal or typical mongoloid variety, and to have a chromosonal count. Results of both tests were normal. It was felt that clinical intuition and psychometric findings were confirmed — that private school was the best placement. Learning materials were programmed to fit the SOI deficits in the hope of some remediation by tying all learning to figural stimuli.

Educationally Handicapped Children. Figure 11-6 (SOI profile) shows typical poor memory responses of the EH — evaluation is poor, semantics across operations is very weak, divergent production is weak.

FIGURE 11-5

BINET PROFILE OF RETARDATION: BRAIN DAMAGE
Tally Sheet for Stanford-Binet (LM) Templates

STRUCTURE OF INTELLECT PROFILE
With a Flow Diagram of the Processes

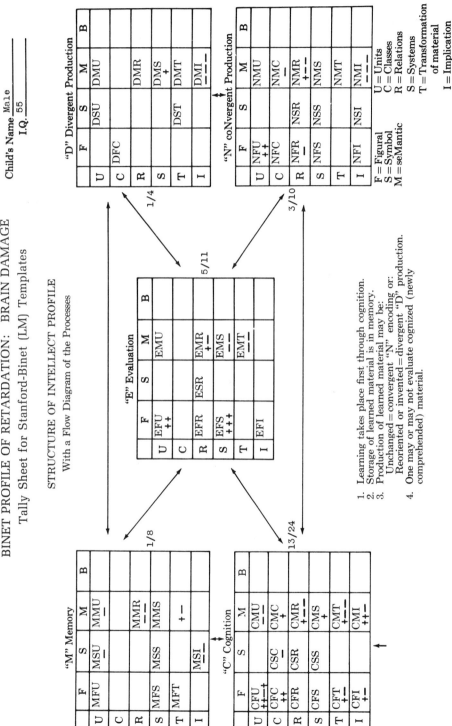

165

FIGURE 11-6

BINET PROFILE OF E.H.: BEHAVIOR PROBLEM

Tally Sheet for Stanford-Binet (LM) Templates

STRUCTURE OF INTELLECT PROFILE
With a Flow Diagram of the Processes

Child's Name **Male**

I.Q. **104**

E.H. Behavior Problem

"C" Cognition

	F	S	M	B
U	CFU		CMU ++ == ++	
C	CFC	CSC ++	CMC	
R	CFR	CSR	CMR __	
S	CFS +	CSS	CMS + __ __	
T	CFT __ +		CMT + __ __	
I	CFI		CMI __ __	

"M" Memory

	F	S	M	B
U	MFU __	MSU __	MMU __	
C				
R			MMR __	
S	MFS ++ ++	MSS __	MMS	
T	MFT			
I	MSI + __			

"E" Evaluation

	F	S	M	B
U	EFU		EMU __ +	
C		ESR		
R	EFR		EMR __ __	
S	EFS		EMS __ __ __	
T			EMT	
I	EFI			

"D" Divergent Production

	F	S	M	B
U		DSU	DMU __	
C	DFC			
R			DMR	
S			DMS __ + __	
T		DST __	DMT __	
I			DMI __	

"N" coNvergent Production

	F	S	M	B
U	NFU	NSU	NMU	
C	NFC		NMC	
R	NFR	NSR	NMR __	
S	NFS	NSS +	NMS	
T			NMT __ __	
I	NFI	NSI ++	NMI __	

F = Figural
S = Symbol
M = seMantic

U = Units
C = Classes
R = Relations
S = Systems
T = Transformation of material
I = Implication

1. Learning takes place first through cognition.
2. Storage of learned material is in memory.
3. Production of learned material may be:
   Unchanged = convergent "N", encoding or:
   Reoriented or invented = divergent "D" production.
4. One may or may not evaluate cognized (newly comprehended) material.

3/10

1/9

3/8

1/7

10/23

FIGURE 11-7

BINET PROFILE OF E.H.: EMOTIONALLY DISTURBED
Tally Sheet for Stanford-Binet (LM) Templates

Child's Name _Female_

I.Q. _96_

E.H. Emotionally disturbed

STRUCTURE OF INTELLECT PROFILE
With a Flow Diagram of the Processes

"M" Memory

	F	S	M	B
U	MFU —	MSU —	MMU —	
C				
R			MMR	
S	MFS ++	MSS —	MMS	
T	MFT			
I		MSI —		

"C" Cognition

	F	S	M	B
U	CFU		CMU ±+±+	
C	CFC	CSC +-	CMC —	
R	CFR	CSR	CMR	
S	CFS —	CSS —	CMS ---	
T	CFT -+±		CMT	
I	CFI +-		CMI +	

"E" Evaluation

	F	S	M	B
U	EFU		EMU +-	
C				
R	EFR	ESR	EMR +-	
S	EFS		EMS --	
T			EMT	
I	EFI			

"D" Divergent Production

	F	S	M	B
U		DSU	DMU —	
C	DFC			
R			DMR +--	
S			DMS	
T		DST +-	DMT +-	
I			DMI	

"N" coNvergent Production

	F	S	M	B
U	NFU		NMU	
C	NFC		NMC	
R	NFR —	NSR	NMR —	
S	NFS +	NSS +	NMS +	
T			NMT +-	
I	NFI	NSI +-	NMI	

Flow fractions: M→E 2/12; C→E 11/26; E 2/7; D 3/7; N 5/11

1. Learning takes place first through cognition.
2. Storage of learned material is in memory.
3. Production of learned material may be:
   Unchanged = convergent "N" encoding; or:
   Reoriented or invented = divergent "D" production.
4. One may or may not evaluate cognized (newly comprehended) material.

F = Figural
S = Symbol
M = seMantic

U = Units
C = Classes
R = Relations
S = Systems
T = Transformation of material
I = Implication

This boy had severe social problems. He was given memory work and a concentrated program in semantics. Ideas rather than vocabulary were stressed. He was required to vocalize and put into written form most of his reading assignments. His individual curriculum acted as an incentive for other class members who participated, following his lead. He gradually became more confident, and behavior problems soon ceased. Academic progress was slower, but was up to grade level at the time of his release from the EH program.

The success of all of the students in this class was due to this teacher's ability to structure work for their individual needs. Her teaching skills, her flexibility, and her personality left no question in the minds of the administrators in this school that her continued success with EH students kept these students from being drop-outs.

Figures 11-7 and 11-8 also typify SOI profiles of educationally handicapped students who seem to have poor memory. Those who are behavior problems usually show deficits in evaluation items. Those who are highly anxious, tense, and insecure usually show weakness in divergent production.

Figure 11-9 shows Binet-SOI responses of a Caucasian boy, age 12, who had been expelled from school and was homebound with special home teaching for one year. He was the only boy of an older mother and father who lived according to a strict religious code. They refused to recognize or admit that the boy had problems, even when he was expelled.

When he returned to be admitted to school he was given a Binet, a Bender-Gestalt, and the Wide Range Achievement Test. The Binet gave a score of 121. He was five years retarded in reading and at grade level in arithmetic. The Bender-Gestalt indicated perceptual problems. A projective interpretation indicated severe anxiety and acting out. Visual examination proved vision to be normal. An EEG showed atypical brain waves, and the neurologist said he had brain damage. He had been expelled for "dirty talk," molesting young girls, and carrying a knife regularly, even when arrested and ordered not to do so.

Note the unusual strengths in the figural and symbolic areas across all operations; note the high number of failures in all five semantic dimensions. Strengths in divergent production indicate items tied in with arithmetic items. His teacher did feel he was creative and reported that his favorite pastime was cooking.

He was placed in an EH class. With the aid of classifying cards (twenty minutes a day, three times a week) and units discrimination tasks on the tachistoscope and Language Master, he was, at the end of one year, reading at only two years below grade level. Semantics and interpretations were concentrated upon daily. Math remained one of his best subjects. Behavioral problems were discussed by the class members once a week under the teacher's guidance. This boy stayed withdrawn for one semester, but later,

FIGURE 11-8

BINET PROFILE OF E.H.: LEADER
Tally Sheet for Stanford-Binet (LM) Templates

Child's Name __Male__
I.Q. __90__
E.H. Leader

STRUCTURE OF INTELLECT PROFILE
With a Flow Diagram of the Processes

"M" Memory   0/6

	F	S	M	B
U	MFU	MSU −	MMU	
C				
R			MMR −	
S	MFS −/−	MSS −	MMS	
T	MFT			
I		MSI		

"C" Cognition   11/20

	F	S	M	B
U	CFU		CMU −+/+++	
C	CFC	CSC ++	CMC	
R	CFR	CSR	CMR	
S	CFS −/−	CSS +	CMS	
T	CFT ++/−		CMT −	
I	CFI +/+		CMI +	

"E" Evaluation   6/8

	F	S	M	B
U	EFU		EMU − −	
C				
R	EFR	ESR	EMR +++/+	
S	EFS		EMS +/−	
T			EMT	
I	EFI			

"D" Divergent Production   4/5

	F	S	M	B
U		DSU	DMU	
C	DFC			
R			DMR	
S			DMS +/−	
T		DST ++	DMT +	
I			DMI	

"N" coNvergent Production   6/9

	F	S	M	B
U	NFU		NMU	
C	NFC		NMC	
R	NFR +	NSR	NMR	
S	NFS	NSS +/−	NMS ++	
T			NMT −	
I	NFI +	NSI +	NMI	

U = Units
C = Classes
R = Relations
S = Systems
T = Transformation of material
I = Implication

F = Figural
S = Symbol
M = seMantic

1. Learning takes place first through cognition.
2. Storage of learned material is in memory.
3. Production of learned material may be:
   Unchanged = convergent "N" encoding; or:
   Reoriented or invented = divergent "D" production.
4. One may or may not evaluate cognized (newly comprehended) material.

FIGURE 11-9

BINET PROFILE OF E.H.: IRREGULAR EEG
Tally Sheet for Stanford-Binet (LM) Templates

STRUCTURE OF INTELLECT PROFILE
With a Flow Diagram of the Processes

Child's Name Male
I.Q. 121 Vocab. 10
E.H. Irregular EEG

Apprehended for molesting and threatening young girls

"D" Divergent Production

	F	S	M	B
U		DSU +	DMU +	
C	DFC +			
R			DMR	
S			DMS -	
T		DST ++	DMT ++	
I			DMI +	

"N" coNvergent Production

	F	S	M	B
U	NFU		NMU	
C	NFC		NMC -	
R	NFR ++	NSR +	NMR +-	
S	NFS +	NSS +	NMS -	
T			NMT --	
I	NFI +	NSI ++	NMI +-	

"E" Evaluation

	F	S	M	B
U	EFU		EMU -	
C				
R	EFR	ESR	EMR === +	
S	EFS		EMS	
T			EMT + - -	
I	EFI +			

"M" Memory

	F	S	M	B
U	MFU +	MSU ++	MMU	
C				
R			MMR +	
S	MFS +++	MSS ++ -	MMS -	
T	MFT -			
I		MSI - +		

"C" Cognition

	F	S	M	B
U	CFU		CMU ++ ===	
C	CFC	CSC ++	CMC	
R	CFR	CSR	CMR - -	
S	CFS ++	CSS +	CMS +	
T	CFT		CMT - -	
I	CFI ++		CMI + -	

Arrows: 8/10, 3/13, 10/18, 11/31

F = Figural
S = Symbol
M = seMantic

U = Units
C = Classes
R = Relations
S = Systems
T = Transformation of material
I = Implication

1. Learning takes place first through cognition.
2. Storage of learned material is in memory.
3. Production of learned material may be:
   Unchanged = convergent "N," encoding or:
   Reoriented or invented = divergent "D," production.
4. One may or may not evaluate cognized (newly comprehended) material.

when discussions were turned to cooking, his hobby, he began to take part in them. He was overly obedient. After a year and a half, he had improved scholastically more than any of the other eleven students in the class. At the end of the second year, however, urges overcame him and he was again reported for threatening younger girls with a knife if they did not allow him to make advances. He was apprehended and placed in a state institution where he now receives psychiatric treatment and medication.

Figure 11-10 is the Binet profile of a girl who was placed in an EH program for two years; her achievement at placement was five years retarded in reading and two years retarded in arithmetic. She shows the typical poor memory, good evaluation pattern, with additional deficits at the units level. Note failures in systems thinking in all operations except divergent production. Her pattern of strength in the more abstract divergent-production tasks, when combined with her strength in cognition and convergent production of transformations, led to an inquiry about her learning predisposition. We discovered upon questioning that she was indeed a motor learner; she said she had to write everything if she wanted to learn it. She then complained vehemently that she would have been a better student if teachers gave her enough time to write everything down in class, but they never gave her time to do so and she knew they thought she was lazy. It was our opinion that this may partially explain her failures in the systems dimension — that being a motor "translator," she was too engrossed with the parts to learn or "see" totalities of the material to be learned. Since she was testing at the upper end of the Binet scale, there were too few figural responses to give more information about her lack of "gestalt" learning ability.

Programmed instruction for this student was slowed down in the EH class. She was given opportunity and time to write everything she had to learn. She spent much time with the Language Master and at the blackboard. By the end of two years she made the greatest gains of all the class members in achievement scores and was scoring at expected levels. She knew she would have to continue writing any material she wanted to integrate into her knowledge, and her success gave her confidence in accepting this fact. She has since begun to study at a nursing school and so far is very pleased. At this writing she has been successful in the nursing program for one semester, but what is more important is her knowledge and acceptance of her specific learning problem. She not only has learned to pace her learning but in accepting her particular predisposition to learning she feels she can live with it and succeed in spite of it.

Gifted Children. Figure 11-11 comes from the Binet responses of a girl age 4.11, whose Binet IQ was 169 and whose WPPSI was 132. Her Winterhaven was normal, but after seeing her SOI profile it was decided to give the girl a Bender because of her failures in the unit items of all operations except cognition. Her motor coordination, otherwise excellent, showed severe persevera-

FIGURE 11-10
BINET PROFILE OF E.H.: MOTOR LEARNER
Tally Sheet for Stanford-Binet (LM) Templates

Child's Name Female
I.Q. 123
E.H. Motor learner
Perceptual difficulty

STRUCTURE OF INTELLECT PROFILE
With a Flow Diagram of the Processes

"D" Divergent Production

	F	S	M	B
U		DSU	DMU −|−	
C	DFC			
R			DMR	
S			DMS ++ +|−	
T		DST ++	DMT +	
I			DMI ++	

8/11

"N" coNvergent Production

	F	S	M	B
U	NFU		NMU	
C	NFC		NMC	
R	NFR −+	NSR	NMR −+	
S	NFS	NSS −|	NMS −|	
T			NMT +++++	
I	NFI +	NSI +	NMI +|−	

8/15

"E" Evaluation

	F	S	M	B
U	EFU		EMU −|−	
C				
R	EFR	ESR +	EMR ++ +	
S	EFS		EMS	
T			EMT	
I	EFI			

3/5

"M" Memory

	F	S	M	B
U	MFU −	MSU −	MMU −+	
C				
R			MMR	
S	MFS +	MSS −	MMS	
T	MFT			
I		MSI −		

2/11

"C" Cognition

	F	S	M	B
U	CFU		CMU ±=++++	
C	CFC	CSC + − −	CMC +	
R	CFR	CSR	CMR	
S	CFS −+	CSS − −	CMS −|−|−|	
T	CFT −+		CMT +++ −	
I	CFI + −		CMI + −	

14/36

F = Figural
S = Symbol
M = seMantic

U = Units
C = Classes
R = Relations
S = Systems
T = Transformation of material
I = Implication

1. Learning takes place first through cognition.
2. Storage of learned material is in memory.
3. Production of learned material may be:
   Unchanged = convergent "N", encoding or:
   Reoriented or invented = divergent "D" production.
4. One may or may not evaluate cognized (newly comprehended) material.

FIGURE 11-11

BINET PROFILE OF GIFTED: BRAIN DAMAGED

Tally Sheet for Stanford-Binet (LM) Templates

STRUCTURE OF INTELLECT PROFILE

With a Flow Diagram of the Processes

Child's Name __Female__
I.Q. __169__
C.A. 4.11
WPSSI 132
Winterhaven Normal

Bender Perseveration and collision

"D" Divergent Production

	F	S	M	B
U		DSU −	DMU −	
C	DFC +			
R			DMR −	
S			DMS	
T		DST	DMT	
I			DMI ++++	

5/8

"N" coNvergent Production

	F	S	M	B
U	NFU −|−		NMU	
C	NFC		NMC +|−	
R	NFR +	NSR	NMR +++	
S	NFS	NSS	NMS	
T			NMT	
I	NFI +|−	NSI	NMI +++	

9/13

"E" Evaluation

	F	S	M	B
U	EFU −	ESR	EMU	
C				
R	EFR	ESR −	EMR ++|−−	
S	EFS +|−		EMS +−−−|−	
T			EMT ++	
I	EFI			

6/14

"M" Memory

	F	S	M	B
U	MFU −|−+	MSU +|−	MMU −	
C				
R			MMR +++	
S	MFS	MSS +	MMS +|−	
T	MFT			
I		MSI ++|		

9/15

"C" Cognition

	F	S	M	B
U	CFU +|+	CSU	CMU == / +++	
C	CFC	CSC	CMC	
R	CFR	CSR	CMR	
S	CFS +	CSS	CMS	
T	CFT ++|−		CMT +−|+−	
I	CFI ++−|−−		CMI ++	

8/10   9/14   17/25

U = Units
C = Classes
R = Relations
S = Systems
T = Transformation of material
I = Implication

F = Figural
S = Symbol
M = seMantic

1. Learning takes place first through cognition.
2. Storage of learned material is in memory.
3. Production of learned material may be:
   Unchanged = convergent "N," encoding or;
   Reoriented or invented = divergent "D" production.
4. One may or may not evaluate cognized (newly comprehended) material.

tion and collisions in the Bender. Normally the Bender would not be given to a child of this age, but it was used here as a confirmatory check for visual dysfunctioning. On the basis of this difficulty and her inability in processing units discriminations, a visual examination was requested. An orthoptics examination showed severe fusion problems.

Note the strengths in transformations and implications across operations. We can conclude she has ability in abstract thinking and has creative potential. Since she has good strengths in the relations dimension (CMR, MMR, NFR, and NMR) and also in the semantic areas of cognition and convergent production, with her visual problem taken care of she will undoubtedly have less trouble in learning visual-motor skills and in reading. If units abilities are now stimulated and recovery achieved, she should work at a gifted level in school.

Figures 11-12 and 11-13 are profiles of gifted children who have been blind from birth. An analysis of Binets of a random sample of blind children from Braille Institute, Los Angeles, showed a distinct grouping of patterns. For those children whose IQ's were under 140, group weaknesses were found in the figural dimension, and nearly all of them showed deficits in the figural dimensions in all operations. Seventy-five percent of them also showed weaknesses in the relations dimension across all operations. (See FIG. 11-12.) The profiles of those students above 140, however, did not show these deficits either in the figural dimension or in the relations dimension, but instead showed individual patterns typical of the non-blind gifted. These patterns have implications for the kinds of tasks which need to be stressed with the blind.

Another group distinction was noted in the SOI profiles of this sample, and that was that the severely anxious and severely disturbed blind students showed extreme deficits in all the divergent-production columns regardless of IQ score.

In an earlier study of gifted children (Meeker, 1968), academically gifted students were matched by IQ score with the creative gifted, all of whom were 98 percentile achievers on the CTMM. Figures 11-14 and 11-15 show the profiles of two of these children who were matched by score and designated academically gifted and creatively gifted.

Figure 11-15 is that of a non-creative gifted child. Ratings on creativity were made by teacher, parents, and psychologist. Note that the divergent-production area is heavily loaded with minuses as are the implications levels across dimensions. One may well ask whether or not this is perhaps a highly anxious child. He was very withdrawn, seemed unusually calm, and answered questions like a computer or robot. The psychologist noted that as questions were asked, methodically measured responses were emitted slowly and deliberately. A four-year follow-up on this child showed that he remained an A student through high school and still very reserved. He did not participate in school affairs but was reliable and became a recipient of good-conduct honors as a senior. Another interesting pattern for him is the number of

FIGURE 11-12

HAYES-BINET PROFILE OF LOW GIFTED: BLIND

Tally Sheet for Stanford-Binet (LM) Templates

STRUCTURE OF INTELLECT PROFILE

With a Flow Diagram of the Processes

Child's Name Female
I.Q. 134 Vocab. 16
MA. 13.10
C.A. 10.4

"M" Memory

	F	S	M	B
U	MFU	MSU +++-	MMU +++	
C				
R			MMR ++--	
S	MFS -	MSS ++ -	MMS +-+	
T	MFT --			
I		MSI +++		

15/23

"C" Cognition

	F	S	M	B
U	CFU		CMU +++ ===---	
C	CFC	CSC +-	CMC	
R	CFR +	CSR +-	CMR ----	
S	CFS	CSS	CMS -	
T	CFT		CMT +	
I	CFI +		CMI +- -	

9/23

"E" Evaluation

	F	S	M	B
U	EFU		EMU -	
C				
R	EFR	ESR	EMR ++-- ==	
S	EFS		EMS ++	
T			EMT	
I	EFI			

5/13

"D" Divergent Production

	F	S	M	B
U		DSU +	DMU +	
C	DFC			
R			DMR --	
S			DMS -	
T		DST +-	DMT +-	
I			DMI +-	

5/11

"N" coNvergent Production

	F	S	M	B
U	NFU	NSU	NMU	
C	NFC		NMC +	
R	NFR -	NSR	NMR +-	
S	NFS	NSS	NMS	
T			NMT ++ ==	
I	NFI	NSI +-	NMI +- -	

6/19

F = Figural
S = Symbol
M = seMantic

U = Units
C = Classes
R = Relations
S = Systems
T = Transformation of material
I = Implication

1. Learning takes place first through cognition.
2. Storage of learned material is in memory.
3. Production of learned material may be:
   Unchanged = convergent "N", encoding or:
   Reoriented or invented = divergent "D" production.
4. One may or may not evaluate cognized (newly comprehended) material.

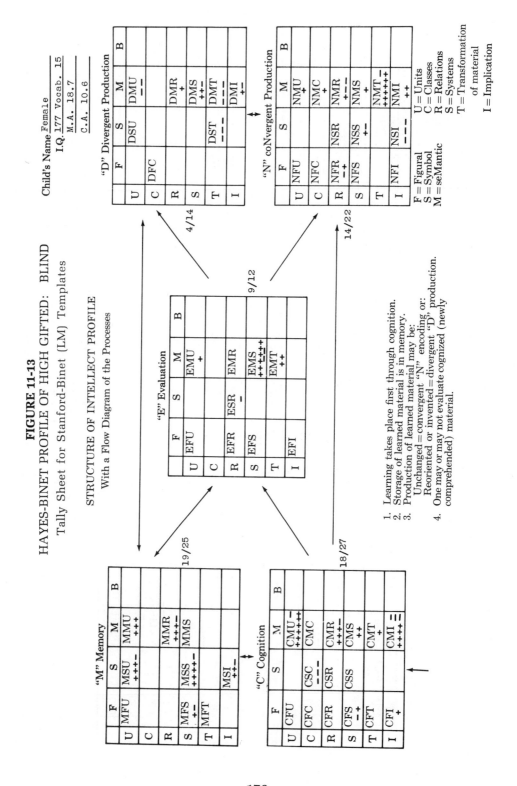

FIGURE 11-13

HAYES-BINET PROFILE OF HIGH GIFTED: BLIND

Tally Sheet for Stanford-Binet (LM) Templates

STRUCTURE OF INTELLECT PROFILE

With a Flow Diagram of the Processes

Child's Name Female

I.Q. 177 Vocab. 15
M.A. 18.7
C.A. 10.6

"D" Divergent Production

	F	S	M	B
U		DSU	DMU − −	
C	DFC			
R			DMR +	
S			DMS ++−	
T		DST − −	DMT − −	
I			DMI −+	

4/14

"N" coNvergent Production

	F	S	M	B
U	NFU		NMU −+	
C	NFC		NMC +	
R	NFR −+	NSR	NMR +−−	
S	NFS	NSS +−	NMS +	
T			NMT +++++++	
I	NFI − −	NSI − −	NMI ++	

14/22

F = Figural   U = Units
S = Symbol   C = Classes
M = seMantic   R = Relations
                  S = Systems
                  T = Transformation
                      of material
                  I = Implication

"E" Evaluation

	F	S	M	B
U	EFU		EMU +	
C		ESR −	EMR	
R	EFR			
S	EFS		EMS +++−+++	
T			EMT ++	
I	EFI			

9/12

"M" Memory

	F	S	M	B
U	MFU	MSU +++−	MMU +++	
C				
R			MMR +++−	
S	MFS +−	MSS +++− −	MMS +++	
T	MFT			
I		MSI ++ −+		

19/25

"C" Cognition

	F	S	M	B
U	CFU		CMU − +++++	
C	CFC	CSC − − −	CMC	
R	CFR	CSR	CMR +++−	
S	CFS − +	CSS	CMS ++	
T	CFT		CMT +	
I	CFI +		CMI = = +++++	

18/27

1. Learning takes place first through cognition.
2. Storage of learned material is in memory.
3. Production of learned material may be:
   Unchanged = convergent "N" encoding or:
   Reoriented or invented = divergent "D" production.
4. One may or may not evaluate cognized (newly
   comprehended) material.

FIGURE 11-14
BINET PROFILE OF GIFTED: CREATIVE LEADER
Tally Sheet for Stanford-Binet (LM) Templates

STRUCTURE OF INTELLECT PROFILE
With a Flow Diagram of the Processes

Child's Name Male
I.Q. 142
Basal 12
C.A. 11.4
Creative leader

"D" Divergent Production

	F	S	M	B
U		DSU	DMU +	
C	DFC			
R			DMR +	
S			DMS +−+	
T		DST +++	DMT ++++	
I			DMI −	

12/13

"N" coNvergent Production

	F	S	M	B
U	NFU		NMU −−	
C	NFC		NMC	
R	NFR +++	NSR +	NMR +=	
S	NFS +	NSS +−	NMS −	
T			NMT +++	
I	NFI	NSI +++	NMI ++−	

15/23

"E" Evaluation

	F	S	M	B
U	EFU		EMU +	
C				
R	EFR	ESR −	EMR + / ++++=	
S	EFS		EMS ++	
T			EMT	
I	EFI +			

9/12

"M" Memory

	F	S	M	B
U	MFU	MSU +−	MMU	
C				
R			MMR +−	
S	MFS +++−	MSS +++−	MMS +	
T	MFT +			
I		MSI ++−		

12/18

"C" Cognition

	F	S	M	B
U	CFU		CMU ++ / +++ ==	
C	CFC	CSC +++	CMC	
R	CFR	CSR	CMR +++−	
S	CFS ++−	CSS +	CMS −−	
T	CFT		CMT −−+	
I	CFI +		CMI ++++−	

20/37

F = Figural
S = Symbol
M = seMantic

U = Units
C = Classes
R = Relations
S = Systems
T = Transformation of material
I = Implication

1. Learning takes place first through cognition.
2. Storage of learned material is in memory.
3. Production of learned material may be:
   Unchanged = convergent "N" encoding, or:
   Reoriented or invented = divergent "D" production.
4. One may or may not evaluate cognized (newly comprehended) material.

FIGURE 11-15

BINET PROFILE OF GIFTED: NON-CREATIVE
Tally Sheet for Stanford-Binet [LM] Templates

STRUCTURE OF INTELLECT PROFILE
With a Flow Diagram of the Processes

Child's Name Male
I.Q. 140

Basal 12
C.A. 11.5

"D" Divergent Production

	F	S	M	B
U		DSU	DMU —	
C	DFC			
R			DMR —	
S			DMS +−	
T		DST	DMT —	
I			DMI —	

"N" coNvergent Production

	F	S	M	B
U	NFU −−	NSU	NMU ++	
C	NFC −		NMC +	
R	NFR −−	NSR +	NMR ++	
S	NFS −	NSS +−	NMS +	
T			NMT +−	
I	NFI −−−	NSI −−−	NMI −−−	

"E" Evaluation

	F	S	M	B
U	EFU	ESR	EMU +	
C				
R	EFR	ESR	EMR ++++ / ==	
S	EFS		EMS +−	
T			EMT	
I	EFI −			

"M" Memory

	F	S	M	B
U	MFU +	MSU ++	MMU	
C				
R			MMR +++	
S	MFS −−	MSS +++−	MMS ++	
T	MFT			
I		MSI +−−		

"C" Cognition

	F	S	M	B
U	CFU	CSU	CMU ++++ / +==	
C	CFC	CSC −−	CMC	
R	CFR	CSR	CMR +−+	
S	CFS −−	CSS +	CMS −++	
T	CFT		CMT +++−	
I	CFI		CMI +−−−	

Arrow labels: 1/10, 9/23, 6/11, 12/19, 16/30

F = Figural
S = Symbol
M = seMantic

U = Units
C = Classes
R = Relations
S = Systems
T = Transformation of material
I = Implication

1. Learning takes place first through cognition.
2. Storage of learned material is in memory.
3. Production of learned material may be:
   Unchanged = convergent "N", encoding; or:
   Reoriented or invented = divergent "D" production.
4. One may or may not evaluate cognized (newly comprehended) material.

failures in the figural dimensions. They have not proved troublesome to him perhaps because high school work is more semantic than figural. The student has consistently worked well in numerical skills and in the more concrete semantic areas.

Figure 11-14, on the other hand, is the profile of a student judged to be creative. It shows strengths in the divergent-production area and strengths in the transformation and implications dimensions. At the time of testing (sixth grade), this boy had ambitions to be a lawyer, although his father was a skilled craftsman. His verbal fluency was rapid, but he needed much work in vocabulary (CMU) and in comprehending abstract ideas (systems of ideas). He was counseled to follow his interest in law and economics by reading *Time* and *Newsweek* magazines, and was guided into debating. He has since become very proficient in forensics and has maintained his leadership. He is very creative in debate, especially in producing transformations of ideas (NMT). He gradually increased his vocabulary through constant reading, although his home was not one where high language concepts were practiced; he has, through perseverance, acquired a dynamic speaking vocabulary. Through the efforts of his counselor, the student, who had taken many honors for his high school in debate, was offered two scholarships by major universities in the area.

Towards Curriculum Planning

What is a deficit? What is a strength? Do I want to teach through a strength or to a strength? Should I teach to a deficit? If we keep in mind the fact that the SOI analysis is obviously only as good as the Binet or WISC, then we can answer these questions by assigning a tentative value to any response. In the Binet any one item accounts for two months of mental age. If a cell in the SOI analysis shows a minus, then that is similar to missing one item in the Binet. Similarly, a strength (plus) is approximate to gaining two months of mental age.

In practice, psychologists using the SOI analyses have answered such questions in the following manner, when SOI assessments have been made on every child who is in a program. Each child has a curriculum based on his intellectual pattern. For children with learning disabilities, it was established that any cell with two minus signs not outweighed by two plus signs constituted a weakness. More than two minus signs is considered a deficit, because it means that the child has failed items totaling four or more months of mental age. The same holds true for a strength. Thus, each individual curriculum format developed is based on a proportion of strengths and weaknesses.

If, as sometimes is the case, there is an equal number of plus signs and minus signs, then color coding will show whether the responses are occurring above, at, or below age level. Since so many items in the Binet are not "pure," it is difficult to assess which one part of an item may be accounting for the success or failure. This can, of course, be done by giving careful attention to the dimensional qualities involved, but until more refined techniques for better SOI evaluations are available, this is all that can be done. The ideal test would, of course, be a factor-analytic, SOI group test which could be used instead of the traditional group maturity or intelligence tests currently in use. Information coming from such a test would eliminate problems involved in a more exact interpretation of derived analyses from individual tests, but until such a group test is developed, we must depend on individual tests and SOI derivatives for individual assessments of exceptional children. Plans are under way for an elementary group SOI test at the University of Southern California, but it is expected that a minimum of five years will be required to standardize and validate the test for school use. However, SOI analyses derived from the Binet and WISC do capitalize on the reliability and validity of these standardized tests. For the present, the skill of the psychologist, his art in clinical assessments, and his understanding of the conceptual meaning of the SOI will enable him to determine what the child in question should be taught and whether this should be taught through his strengths or directly to his deficits. And here, of course, the cooperating teacher will have to temper her best judgment with that of the psychologist.

The standard procedure for programs for the perceptual dysfunctioning or minimally brain damaged (MBD) children includes highly structured lesson plans. This approach is used because "bit" types of steps in programs facilitate learning for these students. Psychologists find that figural or pictorial stimuli are more primitive and are more easily retained (Jenkins, Neale, Deno, 1967). If figural items are weak, and they typically are on MBD with visual problems, materials composed of figural stimuli are used exclusively until growth occurs. Figural material is taught first at a units level, then at a classifications level, next at a relations level, and so on through the vertical order of products through the implications level.

Many teaching materials are composed of figural items. Among them are:

1) Thelma Thurstone, "Learning to Think Series," SRA
2) Dorothea Noble Paul, "Going Places in Reading Readiness"
3) Sullivan's programmed material
4) Valett's psycho-educational programs
5) Frostig's work sheets for perceptual development
6) Upton and Sampson's "Creative Analysis"

It will be necessary for teacher and psychologist to determine which operations and products the figural materials are teaching, at least for the present.

If semantics are weak and figural strong, we rarely present a semantic without its figural counterpart simultaneously. When MFU, MSU, or MMU is weak (two or more minuses) plastic letters and numerals are used to develop memory span. The progression often goes like this: The child holds one letter or numeral, says it (in a later series writes it), then holds it behind his back to say it. The span is then increased by one and the process is repeated with two. With repeated success he may leave the room to write the numerals or letters on a blackboard, thus increasing his memory span in length and time. When memory is weak, the necessary seatwork can be presented to him on the Language Master. At first he sits with the Language Master to see and hear the numerals or letters. His time of response is extended in the same way as prescribed in the format for using plastic numerals and letters. Instead of using plastic numerals and letters, he walks a few steps away from the Language Master before responding. This process extends the memory span by a few seconds. After several sessions in which he makes no errors, his time of response is extended by minutes when he is allowed to go to another room and write a series on the blackboard. Most rooms have limited access to a Language Master, unfortunately, but substitute procedures can be made with 5x7 cards. In this case the teacher must structure each bit of information for the student. Such a situation becomes an individual tutorial session. The Language Master can be replaced by a teaching aid or a top student, of course, thus freeing the teacher, but independence in work habits do not eventuate as they do with using the Language Master. The important task, of course, is the stretching of the memory span one way or another.

12

Summary

Education has needed a formal theory of intelligence. It has never had one. Curriculum has never been organized according to a theory of human intellectual functioning. As educators we accept the fact that the child's job for at least twelve years is to learn. We know that his needs represent our major educational goals, and that the possession of intellectual adequacy is indirectly related to the development of a wholesome self-concept. We know that if the child is failing, the system is failing.

We can no longer be satisfied with the notion that intelligence is a simplicity which can be expressed quantitatively as a unity. We need to ask: Intelligence? In what area?

Assessment of intellectual ability has served as a means of predicting academic performance and often even academic types of children. When children of average ability fail to learn, however, an IQ index neither explains nor accounts for their failure. This book has shown how differential intellectual assessments can, by means of a derived SOI profile, be made to give meaning and validity to academic expectancy indices. These differential assessments have curricular implications because they set up guidelines within a theory of intelligence which, once available to the teacher, enable her to construct creatively and comfortably individual programs for development and remediation within her personal fund of instructional materials.

This plan implies a training for competency which will also have a beneficial effect on self-concept. The profiles offer parameters for material to train abilities; they offer a basis for individualized teaching.

183

Primarily this book has attempted to interpret a complex model of intelligence. Its secondary purpose has been to show that cognitive therapy can be accomplished within the domain of the school, for it is in the schools that learning and social problems are most often detected. Toward this latter purpose, directions for a way of planning curriculum are sketched so that individual and group strengths and deficits are discovered and correspondingly taught. The materials are well known to the teacher. What he is not familiar with is a method of organizing teaching experiences so they will best benefit his students. Any specific course of study can be organized so that children receive practice in all of the major operations. If the avowed purpose of education is to make changes in the knowledge funds of students, then we need to be sure that we know what the structure of knowledge is and what learning is expected. Then it becomes our obligation as educators to expose students to these intellectual experiences. Such a situation need no longer be a dream so long as we know what that expected knowledge is.

Educational planning for students admitted to special classes, whether gifted, mentally retarded, educationally handicapped, or neurologically or physically impaired, can now be rooted in a theory of human intelligence. The planning comes from those same behavior samplings which appeared on the tests by which placement was made. One section in the book defines SOI abilities and describes the abilities most commonly being tested by traditional education tests. There are also limited but specific curriculum suggestions for each ability. How individual diagnoses relate to individual curriculum planning constitutes another section. Examples of each are given by way of explication. Another section discusses how organic and intellectual deficits derived from test to test can be confirmed, and how SOI profiles may serve as bases for programmed learning is made explicit.

A small part of the book is devoted to discussing the SOI as an information-processing model, and a schematic representation of acculturated abilities is outlined; this is perhaps the most speculative portion of the book, for it makes a tentative collation of areas of psychological inquiries in order to show how percepts may be related to the development of training materials and to the acquisition of concepts.

Such an attempt may be presumptive in that it is a look at the whole picture. To relate the huge body of experimental study in psychology by looking at modal inputs as they may be processed for the expected knowledge to be arrived at is unquestionably only a beginning.

This book is a beginning.

Bibliography

Abt, C., "Game Learning and Disadvantaged Groups," Abt. Associates, Inc., 1965; Systems Development Corporation, Santa Monica, California, 1968, 1-4.

———, "An Introduction to Educational Games," Abt. Associates, Inc., 1965; Systems Development Corporation, Santa Monica, California, 1968, 1-4.

———, "Games for Learning," The Social Studies Curriculum Program, Occasional Paper No. 7, 1966, 1-24.

Anastasi, Anne, *Psychological Testing*. New York: The Macmillan Company, 1954.

Andrew, Dorothy M. and D. G. Paterson, *Minnesota Clerical Test: Manual*. New York: Psychological Corporation.

Barron, F., "The Creative Individual," CERGA Conference Address, Los Angeles State College, 1959.

Barron, F., *Creativity and Psychological Health*. Princeton, N. J.: D. Van Nostrand Company, 1963.

Bender, Lauretta, "A Visual Motor Gestalt Test and its Clinical Use," *American Orthopsychiatric Association, Research Monograph*, No. 3 (1938), 176.

Bennett, G. K., *Test of Mechanical Comprehension, Form AA: Manual*. New York: Psychological Corporation, 1951. (a)

———, *Test of Mechanical Comprehension, Form BB: Manual*. New York: Psychological Corporation, 1951. (b)

———, H. Seashore, and A. G. Wesman, *Differential Aptitude Tests: Manual*, 2nd ed. New York: Psychological Corporation, 1952.

Berko, J., "The Child's Learning of English Morphology," *Word, 14* (1958), 150-177.

Bijou, S., "A Child Study Laboratory on Wheels," *Child Development, 29* (1958), 425-27.

Binet, A., *Les Idées modernes sur les enfants*. Paris: *Flammarion*, 1909.

———, and V. Henri, "La Psychologie individuelle," *Anée psychologique, 2* (1896), 411-65.

185

————, and Th. Simon, "Méthodes nouvelles pour le diagnostic du niveau intel-lectuel des anormaux," *Anée psychologique, 11* (1905), 191-244.

Blake, P., N. Tiber, M. Kogus, and M. Mahon, "The Effects of Single and Multiple Experimenter Conditions on the Acquisition and Generalization of Operantly Conditioned Verbal Responses in Autistic Children." Unpublished paper, 1966.

Bonsall, Marcella R., and Mary M. Meeker, "Structure-of-Intellect Components in the Stanford-Binet." Unpublished paper, Los Angeles City Schools, 1963.

Brown, R., *Words and Things*. New York: Free Press, 1958.

Brown, S. W., "Semantic-Memory and Creative (Divergent-Production) Abilities of Senior-high-school Students." Unpublished doctoral dissertation, University of Southern California, 1966.

Brown, S. W., J. P. Guilford, and R. Hoepfner, "A Factor Analysis of Semantic-Memory Abilities," *Reports from the Psychological Laboratory, University of Southern California,* No. 37, 1966.

Bruner, J. S., J. J. Goodnow, and G. A. Austin, *A Study of Thinking*. New York: John Wiley & Sons, Inc., 1956.

Buros, O. K., (ed.), *Fifth Mental Measurements Yearbook*. Highland Park, N.J.: Gryphon Press, 1959.

Carlson, D. C. and C. E. Meyers, "Language, Memory, and Figural Ability Hypotheses in Retardates of Mental Age Four," *State of California Department of Mental Hygiene, Bureau of Research,* No. 430, 1967.

Cattell, R. B., "Classical and Standard Score IQ Standardization of the I.P.A.T. Culture-Free Intelligence Scale 2," *Journal of Consulting Psychology, 15* (1951), 154-59.

Cattell, R. B. and A. K. S. Cattell, *Handbook for the Individual or Group Culture-Free Intelligence Test: Scale 2*. Champaign, Ill.: Institute for Personality and Ability Testing, 1949.

Christal, R. E., "Factor Analytic Study of Visual Memory," *Psychological Monographs, 72* (1958), Whole No. 466.

Christensen, P. R., "The Function Sharing Approach to Research on Joint Man-Machine Intelligence," Systems Development Corporation, Santa Monica, California, 1963.

Cronbach, L. J., *Essentials of Psychological Testing*. New York: Harper & Row, Publishers, 1960.

Children's Highlights, W. Barbe (ed.), Columbus, Ohio: Highlights for Children, Inc.

CTMM, "California Test of Mental Maturity," *(See* Sullivan, Clark, and Tiegs).

DAT, "Differential Aptitude Tests," *(See* Bennett, Seashore, and Wesman).

DAT Minnesota Clerical Test *(See* Andrew and Paterson).

Davis, A. and K. Eells, *Davis-Eells Games: A Test of General Intelligence. Directions for Administering Primary A and Elementary A*. Yonkers-on-Hudson, N.Y:. World Book Co., 1953. (a)

————, *Davis-Eells Games: Davis-Eells Test of General Intelligence or Problem-Solving Ability, Manual*. Yonkers-on-Hudson, N.Y.: World Book Co., 1953. (b)

Dunham, J. L., J. P. Guilford, and R. Hoepfner, "Abilities for Dealing with Classes and Learning Concepts," *Reports from the Psychological Laboratory, University of Southern California,* No. 39, 1966.

ETS, "Educational Testing Service," *(See* French, Ekstrom, and Price).

Fantz, R. L., "Visual Perception and Experience in Early Infancy." Unpublished paper presented at the Social Science Research Council Conference, University of Minnesota, 1965.

Feldman, B., Redondo Beach Elementary School District, Redondo Beach, California. "Structure-of-Intellect Factors Correlated with Reading Achievement," Unpublished doctoral dissertation, University of Southern California, 1968.

Fernald, Grace M. *(See* Healy and Fernald).

Flavell, J. H., *The Developmental Psychology of Jean Piaget.* Princeton, N. J.: D. Van Nostrand Company, Inc., 1963.

Fleishman, E. A., M. M. Roberts, and M. P. Friedman, "A Factor Analysis of Aptitude and Proficiency Measures in Radiotelegraphy," *Journal of Applied Psychology, 42,* (1958), 129-137.

French, J. L., *The Pictorial Test of Intelligence, Ages 3-8.* New York: Houghton Mifflin Company, 1964.

French, J. W., Ruth B. Ekstrom, and L. A. Price, *Kit of Reference Tests for Cognitive Factors.* Princeton, N.J.: Educational Testing Service, 1963.

Frostig, Marianne, *Developmental Tests of Visual Perception,* 2nd ed. Palo Alto, Calif.: Consulting Psychologists Press, 1961.

Gallagher, J. J., *Teaching the Gifted Child.* Boston: Allyn Bacon Co., 1964.

————, and M. J. Aschner, *A Preliminary Report on Analyses of Classroom Interaction.* Urbana, Ill.; University of Illinois, Bureau of Educational Research, 1963.

Gesell, A., and F. Ilg, *The Child from Five to Ten.* New York: Harper & Row, Publishers, 1946.

Getzels, J. W., and P. W. Jackson, *Creativity and Intelligence.* New York: John Wiley & Sons, Inc., 1961.

Gillingham, Anna, and Bessie Stillman, *Remedial Training for Children with Specific Disability in Reading, Spelling, and Penmanship.* Cambridge, Mass.: Educators Publishing Service, Inc., 1960.

Gowan, J. C., and G. D. Demos, *The Education and Guidance of the Ablest.* Springfield, Ill.: Charles C. Thomas, 1964.

Guilford, J. P., "The Structure of Intellect." *Psychological Bulletin, 52* (1956), 267-293.

————, "Intelligence — 1965 Model." *American Psychologist, 21,* 1 (1966), 20-26.

————, *The Nature of Human Intelligence.* New York: McGraw-Hill Book Company, 1967.

————, R. M. Berger, and P. R. Christensen, "A Factor-Analytic Study of Planning. I. Hypotheses and Description of Tests," *Reports from the Psychological Laboratory, University of Southern California,* No. 10, 1954.

————, and P. R. Christensen, "A Factor-Analytic Study of Verbal Fluency," *Reports from the Psychological Laboratory, University of Southern California,* No. 17, 1956.

————, J. W. Frick, P. R. Christensen, and P. R. Merrifield, "A Factor-Analytic Study of Flexibility in Thinking," *Reports from the Psychological Laboratory, University of Southern California,* No. 18, 1957.

————, and R. Hoepfner, "Structure-of-Intellect Tests and Factors," *Reports from the Psychological Laboratory, University of Southern California,* No. 36, 1966.

————, N. W. Kettner, and P. R. Christensen, "A Factor-Analytic Study Across the Domains of Reasoning, Creativity, and Evaluation. I. Hypotheses and Description of Tests," *Reports from the Psychological Laboratory, University of Southern California,* No. 11, 1954.

————, N. W. Kettner, and P. R. Christensen, "A Factor-Analytic Investigation of the Factor Called General Reasoning," *Reports from the Psychological Laboratory, University of Southern California,* No. 14, 1955.

————, P. R. Merrifield, P. R. Christensen, and J. W. Frick, "An Investigation of Symbolic Factors of Cognition and Convergent Production," *Reports from the Psychological Laboratory, University of Southern California,* No. 23, 1960.

————, R. C. Wilson, P. R. Christensen, and D. J. Lewis, "A Factor-Analytic Study of Creative Thinking. I. Hypotheses and Description of Tests," *Reports from the Psychological Laboratory, University of Southern California,* No. 4, 1951.

Higashino, S. M. and A. J. Moss, "Capillary Microscopy in Cystic Fibrosis. Congenital Heart Disease and Mongolism," *American Journal of Diseases of Children, 113* (1967), 439.

Hayes, S. P., "A Second Test Scale for the Mental Measurement of the Visually Handicapped," *Outlook for the Blind, 36* (1942), 225-230.

————, "A Second Test Scale for the Mental Measurement of the Visually Handicapped," *Outlook for the Blind, 37* (1943), 37-41.

Healy, W., and Grace M. Fernald, "Tests for Practical Mental Classification," *Psychological Monographs, 13,* 2 (1911), 54.

Henmon-Nelson, *The Henmon-Nelson Tests of Mental Ability, Revised Edition.* New York: Houghton Mifflin Company, 1961.

Hildreth, Gertrude H. and N. L. Griffiths, *Metropolitan Readiness Tests: Directions for Administering and Scoring.* Yonkers-on-Hudson, N. Y.: World Book Co.

Hiskey, M. S., *Nebraska Test of Learning Aptitude for Young Deaf Children: Manual.* Lincoln, Nebr.: University of Nebraska Department of Educational and Psychological Measurement, 1941.

Hoepfner, R., J. P. Guilford, and P. R. Merrifield, "A Factor Analysis of the Symbolic-Evaluation Abilities," *Reports from the Psychological Laboratory, University of Southern California,* No. 33, 1964.

————, and J. P. Guilford, "Figural, Symbolic, and Semantic Factors of Creative Potential in Ninth-Grade Students," *Reports from the Psychological Laboratory, University of Southern California,* No. 35, 1965.

Hollow, Carl, *The Hollow Square Scale Test.* Pennsylvania Hospital, Philadelphia.

Horn, C. C., *Horn Art Aptitude Inventory: Preliminary Form, 1944 Revision, Manual.* Rochester, N.Y.: Office of Educational Research, Rochester Institute of Technology, 1944.

Hudson, Liam, *Contrary Imaginations.* London: Methuen and Company, 1966.

Hunt, Clifton and Robert Benoit, "The Hunt and Benoit Interest Test, Habit," on file with the Bureau of Public Assistance, County of Los Angeles.

Inge, W. M., *Splendor in the Grass.* New York: Bantam Books, Inc., 1961.

Inhelder, Bärbel, and Jean Piaget, *The Growth of Logical Thinking from Childhood to Adolescence.* Basic Books, Inc., Publishers, 1958.

ITPA, "Illinois Test of Psycholinguistic Abilities," *(See* McCarthy and Kirk).

Jastak, J., "A Rigorous Criterion of Feeblemindedness," *Journal of Abnormal Social Psychology, 44* (1939), 367-68.

Jastak, J., and S. Bijou, *Wide Range Achievement Test, 1946 Edition.* New York: Psychological Corporation.

Jenkins, Joseph, Dan Neale, and Stan Deno, "Differential Memory for Pictures and Word Stimuli," *Journal of Educational Psychology, 58,* No. 5 (1967), 303-307.

Karlin, J. E., "A Factorial Study of Auditory Function," *Psychometrika, 7* (1942), 251-279.

Kelley, H. P., "Memory Abilities: A Factor Analysis," *Psychometric Monographs,* No. 11, 1964.

Lee, J. Murray, and Willis Clarke, *Reading Readiness Test.* Los Angeles: California Test Bureau, a Division of McGraw-Hill Book Company, 1962 Revision.

Leiter, R. G., "The Leiter International Performance Scale," *University of Hawaii Bulletin, 15,* No. 7 (1936), 42.

_____, *Part II of the Manual for the 1948 Revision of the Leiter International Performance Scale.* Washington: Psychological Service Center Press, 1952. (Test now published by C. H. Stoelting Co.)

Loeffler, E. J., "An Extension and Partial Replication of Meyers, *et al.,* Primary Abilities at Mental Age Six," Paper read at Society for Research in Child Development, University of California — Berkeley, 1963.

Lorge, I., and Robert L. Thorndike, *The Lorge-Thorndike Intelligence Tests.* New York: Houghton Mifflin Company, 1954-62.

Los Angeles County Social Studies Unit, *Home.* Los Angeles: Los Angeles County, Curriculum Department, 1963.

Lovaas, O., "Cue Properties of Words: The Control of Operant Responding by Rate and Content of Verbal Operants," *Child Development, 35,* No. 1 (1964), 245-256.

Lovaas, O. I., G. Freitag, M. I. Kinder, D. B. Rubenstein, B. Shaeffer, and J. B. Simmons, *Experimental Studies in Childhood Schizophrenia, II and III.* Los Angeles: UCLA Medical School, 1964.

Luke, F., *Many Pennies.* New York: Golden Press, Inc., 1964.

Meeker, Mary, "The NSWP Behavior Samplings in the Binet," Paper presented at the American Psychological Association, Philadelphia, 1963.

_____, "A Procedure for Relating Stanford-Binet Behavior Samplings to Guilford's Structure of the Intellect. *Journal of School Psychology, 3,* No. 3 (1965) 26-36. (a)

————, "Project Headstart," Unpublished study, Los Angeles City Schools, Division of Research, 1965. (b)

————, "Immediate Memory Factors and School Achievement in Ninth Grade Boys," Unpublished doctoral dissertation submitted to *Journal of Ortho-Psychiatry* by M. Meeker and C. E. Meyers, University of Southern California, 1966.

————, "An Evaluation of the Educational Handicapped Program: The Measurables and the Unmeasurables," Special Child Publications, *Educational Therapy II,* 1968. (a)

————, "Differential Syndromes of Giftedness, a 4-Year Follow-up," *Journal of Special Education, 2,* No. 2, Winter, 1968. (b)

Meeker, Mary M., and Marcella R. Bonsall, "Structure of Intellect Components in the Stanford-Binet," Unpublished mimeographed paper, Los Angeles City Schools, 1963.

Merrifield, P. R., "Comparison of NSWP Scores and Other Measures of Aptitudes," American Psychological Association Symposium, Philadelphia, 1963.

Merrifield, P. R., J. P. Guilford, P. R. Christensen, and J. W. Frick, "A Factor-Analytic Study of Problem-Solving Abilities," *Reports from the Psychological Laboratory, University of Southern California,* No. 22, 1960.

Metropolitan Reading Test *(See* Hildreth and Griffiths).

Meyers, C. E., "What the ITPA Measures: A Synthesis of Factor Analytic Studies," Paper presented at AAMD, 1968. Study made at Pacific State Hospital, Pomona, California.

————, H. F. Dingman, R. E. Orpet, E. G. Sitkei, and C. A. Watts, "Four Ability-Factor Hypotheses at Three Preliterate Levels in Normal and Retarded Children," *Monograph of the Society for Research in Child Development," 29,* 5 (1948), 80.

————, R. E. Orpet, A. A. Attwell, and H. F. Dingman, "Primary Mental Abilities at Mental Age Six," *Monograph of the Society for Research in Child Development, 27,* 1 (1962), 40.

————, E. G. Sitkei, and C. A. Watts, "Further Ability Factor Hypotheses at Six Years," Unpublished study, Socio-Behavioral Laboratory, Pacific State Hospital, Pomona, California, 1966.

Miller, W. S., *Manual for the Miller Analogies Test, Form G.* New York: Psychological Corporation, 1947.

Minnesota Tests of Creativity for Children *(See* Torrance).

McCarthy, J. J., and S. A. Kirk, *The Construction, Standardization, and Statistical Characteristics of the Illinois Test of Psycholinguistic Abilities.* Urbana, Ill.: Institute for Research on Exceptional Children, University of Illinois, 1963.

McCartin, Sr. Rose Amata, and C. E. Meyers, "An Exploration of Six Semantic Factors at First Grade," *Multivariate Behavioral Research, 1* (1966), 74-94.

McGuire, Lenore, "The Influence of the Unique Aspect of Blindness on the Development of Blind Children," Unpublished doctoral dissertation, University of Southern California, 1968.

Nihira, K., J. P. Guilford, R. Hoepfner, and P. R. Merrifield, "A Factor-Analysis of the Semantic-Evaluation Abilities," *Reports from the Psychological Laboratory, University of Southern California,* No. 32, 1964.

Orpet, R. E., and C. E. Meyers, "Six Structure-of-Intellect Hypotheses in Six-Year-Old Children," *Journal of Educational Psychology, 57* (1966), 341-46.

O'Sullivan, Maureen, J. P. Guilford, and R. deMille, "The Measurement of Social Intelligence," *Reports from the Psychological Laboratory, University of Southern California,* No. 34, 1965.

Paul, Dorothea, "Going Places in Reading Readiness," in *New Reading Skill Text Series.* Columbus, Ohio: Charles E. Merrill Publishing Co., 1964.

Peabody Picture Vocabulary, American Guidance Service, Publishers Building Circle, Pines, Minnesota.

Peter, Laurence J., *Prescriptive Teaching.* New York: McGraw-Hill Book Company, 1965.

Petersen, H., J. P. Guilford, R. Hoepfner, and P. R. Merrifield, "Determination of 'Structure-of-Intellect' Abilities Involved in Ninth-Grade Algebra and General Mathematics," *Reports from the Psychological Laboratory, University of Southern California,* No. 31, 1963.

Piaget, J., "The Genetic Approach to the Psychology of Thought," *Journal of Educational Psychology, 52* (1961), 275-281. (a)

Piaget, J., *Les Mechanismes perceptifs.* Paris: Presses Univers. de France, 1961. (b)

Piaget, J., "Le Developpement des perceptions en fonction de l'age," in P. Fraisse and J. Piaget (eds), *Traite de psychologies experimentals, VI. La Perception.* Paris: Presses Univers. de France, 1963.

Pintner, R., and D. J. Paterson, *A Scale of Performance Tests.* New York: Appleton-Century-Crofts, 1917.

Porteus, S. D., *Guide to Porteus Maze Test.* Vineland, N.J.: The Training School, 1924.

_____, *Maze Tests and Mental Differences.* Vineland, N.J.: The Training School, 1933.

_____, *The Porteus Maze Test and Intelligence.* Palo Alto, Calif.: Pacific Books, Publishers, 1950.

Randsepp, E., "Testing for Creativity," a reprint from *Machine Design.* Cleveland, Ohio: Penton Publishing Co., May 27, June 10, June 24, 1965.

Rulon, P. J., "A Semantic Test of Intelligence, STI-1952," *Proceedings, 1952 Invitational Conference on Testing Problems,* Educational Testing Service, 84-92.

Russell, D. H., *Children's Thinking.* Boston, Mass.: Ginn and Company, 1956.

Saetveit, J. G., D. Lewis, and C. E. Seashore, "*Revision* of the Seashore Measures of Musical Talents," *University of Iowa Stud., Aims Progr. Res.,* No. 65, 1940.

Schmadel, Elnora, "The Relation of Creative Thinking Abilities to School Achievement," Unpublished doctoral dissertation, University of Southern California, 1960.

Seashore, C. E., D. Lewis, and J. G. Saetveit, *Manual of Instructions and Interpretations for the Seashore Measures of Musical Talents (1937 Revision)*. Camden, N. J.: RCA Victor Division, Radio Corporation of America, 1942. (Now published and distributed by the Psychological Corporation.)

Shaffer, G. W., and R. S. Lazarus, *Fundamental Concepts in Clinical Psychology*. New York: McGraw-Hill Book Company, 1952.

Sheridan Psychological Services, Box 837, Beverly Hills, California.

Sitkei, G., "Comparative Structure of Intellect in Middle and Lower Class Four-Year-Old Children of Two Ethnic Groups," Unpublished doctoral dissertation, University of Southern California, 1966.

Skinner, B. F., *Science and Human Behavior*. New York: The Macmillan Company, 1953.

Skinner, B. F., *Verbal Behavior*. New York: Appleton-Century-Crofts, 1957.

Splendor in the Grass (See Inge).

SRA New Math Series, 259 East Erie, Chicago, Illinois.

SRA Greater Cleveland Math Series, State of California.

Stott, L., and Rachel S. Ball, *Evaluation of Infant and Preschool Mental Tests*. Detroit: Merrill Palmer Institute, 1963.

————, "Infant Preschool Mental Tests: Review and Evaluation," *SCRD Monographs*, Serial No. 101, *30*, No. 3, 1965.

Sullivan Associates, *Programmed Reading, Webster Division*. New York: McGraw-Hill Book Company, 1963.

Sullivan, Elizabeth T., W. W. Clark, and Ernest W. Tiegs, *California Test of Mental Maturity, 1963 Revision*. Monterey, Calif.: California Test Bureau.

Tenopyr, Mary, "Symbolic Memory Tests as Predictors of High-School Grades," Unpublished doctoral dissertation, University of Southern California, 1966.

Tenopyr, Mary, J. P. Guilford, and R. Hoepfner, "A Factor Analysis of Symbolic Memory Abilities," *Reports from the Psychological Laboratory, University of Southern California*, No. 38, 1966.

Thurstone, L. L., "A Factorial Study of Perception," *Psychometric Monographs*, No. 4, 1944.

Thurstone, Thelma G., *Learning to Think Series*. Chicago: Science Research Associates, Inc., 1967.

Torrance, E. P., and others, "Minnesota Studies of Creative Thinking in the Early Years," (mimeographed) Minneapolis: University of Minnesota, College of Education, Bureau of Educational Research, 1960.

Torrance, E. P., and J. C. Gowan, "The Reliability of the Minnesota Tests of Creativity," (mimeographed), Minneapolis: University of Minnesota, Bureau of Educational Research, 1963.

Upton, A., *Design for Thinking*. Palo Alto, Calif.: Stanford University Press, 1959.

Upton, A., and R. W. Samson, *Creative Analysis*. New York: Dutton & Co., 1963.

Valett, R. E., "The Remediation of Learning Disabilities," *A Handbook of Psycho-Educational Resource Programs*." Palo Alto, Calif.: Fearon Publishers, Inc., 1967.

Watson, J. S., "Memory and Contingency Analysis in Infant Learning," Presented at the Merrill-Palmer Institute Conference on Research and Testing of Infant Development, 1966.

✳Watson, R., "Psychology: A Prescriptive Science," *American Psychologist, 22,* No. 6, 1967.

Wechsler, D., "Cognitive, Conative, and Non-Intellective Intelligence," *American Psychologist, 5* (1950), 78-83.

Westcott, A. M., and James A. Smith, *Creative Teaching of Mathematics in the Elementary School.*

✗ Wilson, M. P., "The Relation of Sense of Humor to Creativity, Intelligence, and Achievement," Unpublished doctoral dissertation, University of Southern California, 1968.

WRAT, "Wide Range Achievement Test" *(See* Jastak and Bijou).

Winterhaven Test

Suggested Readings for SOI Validations at Younger Age Levels

McCartin, Sr. Rose Amata, "An Exploration of Six Semantic Factors at First Grade, "*Multivariate Behavioral Research, 1* (1966), 74-94.

Meyers, C. E., R. E. Orpet, and A. A. Atwell, "Psychometric Examination as a Standardized Situation Yielding Personality Data," *Training School Bulletin, 61,* No. 2 (1964), 97-101.

Orpet, R. E., and C. E. Meyers, "Factorially Established Rubrics of Observations of Test Behavior," *Journal of Clinical Psychology, 19,* No. 3 (1963), 292-94.

Glossary

Definitions of Categories in the Structure of Intellect

OPERATIONS

Major kinds of intellectual activities or processes; things that the organism does with the raw materials of information, information being defined as "that which the organism discriminates."

C *Cognition.* Immediate discovery, awareness, rediscovery, or recognition of information in various forms; comprehension or understanding.

M *Memory.* Retention or storage, with some degree of availability, of information in the same form it was committed to storage and in response to the same cues in connection with which it was learned.

D *Divergent Production.* Generation of information from given information, where the emphasis is on variety and quantity of output from the same source. Likely to involve what has been called *transfer.* This operation is most clearly involved in aptitudes of creative potential.

N *coNvergent Production.* Generation of information from given information, where the emphasis is on achieving unique or conventionally accepted best outcomes. It is likely the given (cue) information fully determines the response.

E *Evaluation.* Reaching decisions or making judgments concerning criterion satisfaction (correctness, suitability, adequacy, desirability, etc.) of information.

CONTENTS

Broad classes or types of information discriminable by the organism.

F *Figural.* Information in concrete form, as perceived or as recalled possibly in the form of images. The term "figural" minimally implies figure-ground perceptual organization. Visual spatial information is figural. Different sense modalities may be involved; e.g., visual kinesthetic.

S *Symbolic.* Information in the form of denotative signs, having no significance in and of themselves, such as letters, numbers, musical notations, codes, and words, when meanings and form are not considered.

M seMantic.   Information in the form of meanings to which words commonly become attached, hence most notable in verbal communication but not identical with words. Meaningful pictures also often convey semantic information.

B Behavioral.   Information, essentially non-verbal, involved in human interactions where the attitudes, needs, desires, moods, intentions, perceptions, thoughts, etc., of other people and of ourselves are involved.

PRODUCTS

The organization that information takes in the organism's processing of it.

U Units.   Relatively segregated or circumscribed items of information having "thing" character. May be close to Gestalt psychology's "figure on a ground."

C Classes.   Conceptions underlying sets of items of information grouped by virtue of their common properties.

R Relations.   Connections between items of information based on variables or points of contact that apply to them. Relational connections are more meaningful and definable than implications.

S Systems.   Organized or structured aggregates of items of information; complexes of interrelated or interacting parts.

T Transformations.   Changes of various kinds (redefinition, shifts, or modification) of existing information or in its function.

I Implications.   Extrapolations of information, in the form of expectancies, predictions, known or suspected antecedents, concomitants, or consequences. The connection between the given information and that extrapolated is more general and less definable than a relational connection.

Index

Index